DIWALI

COLORING BOOK FOR KIDS

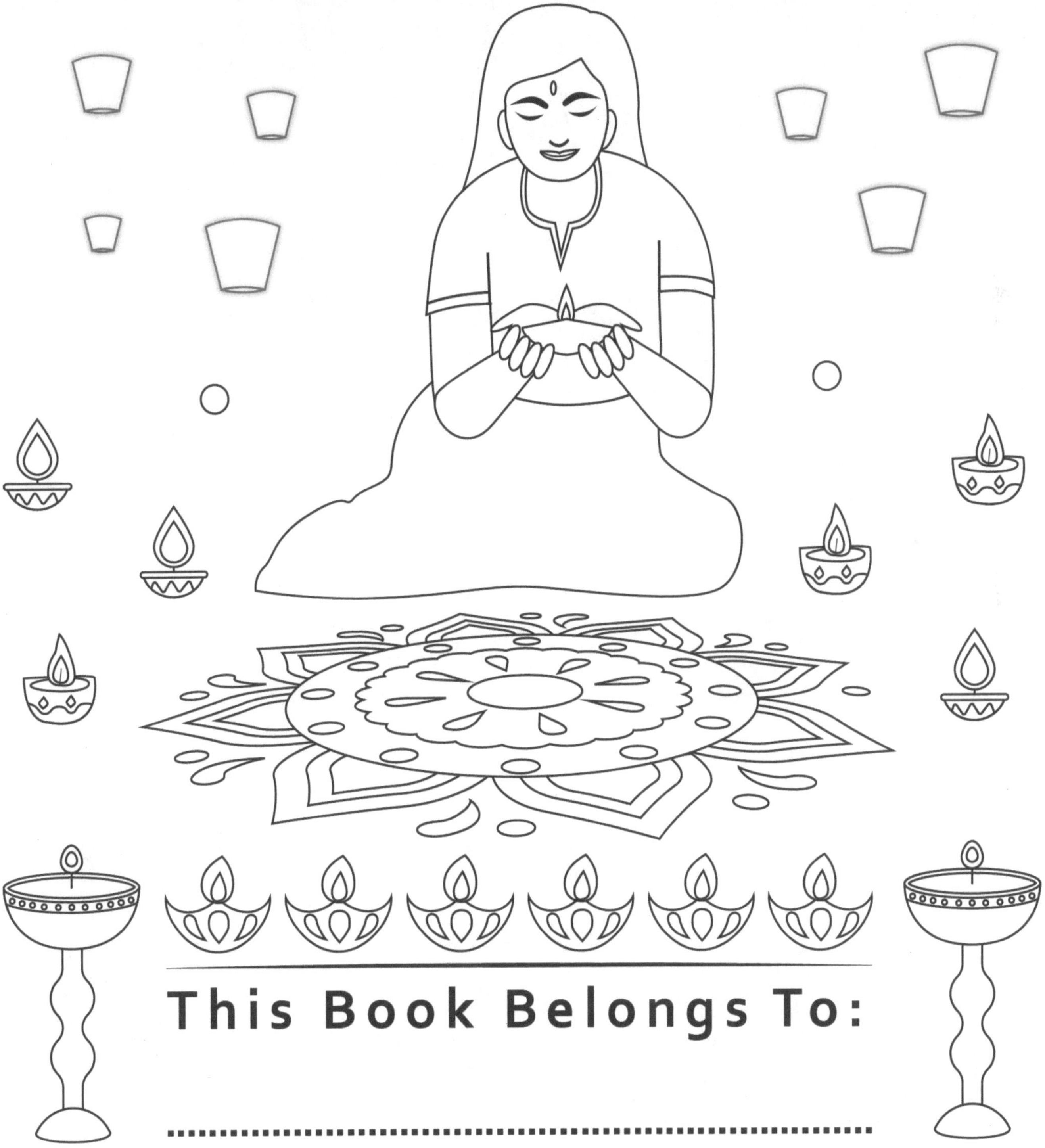

This Book Belongs To:

....

COLOR TEST

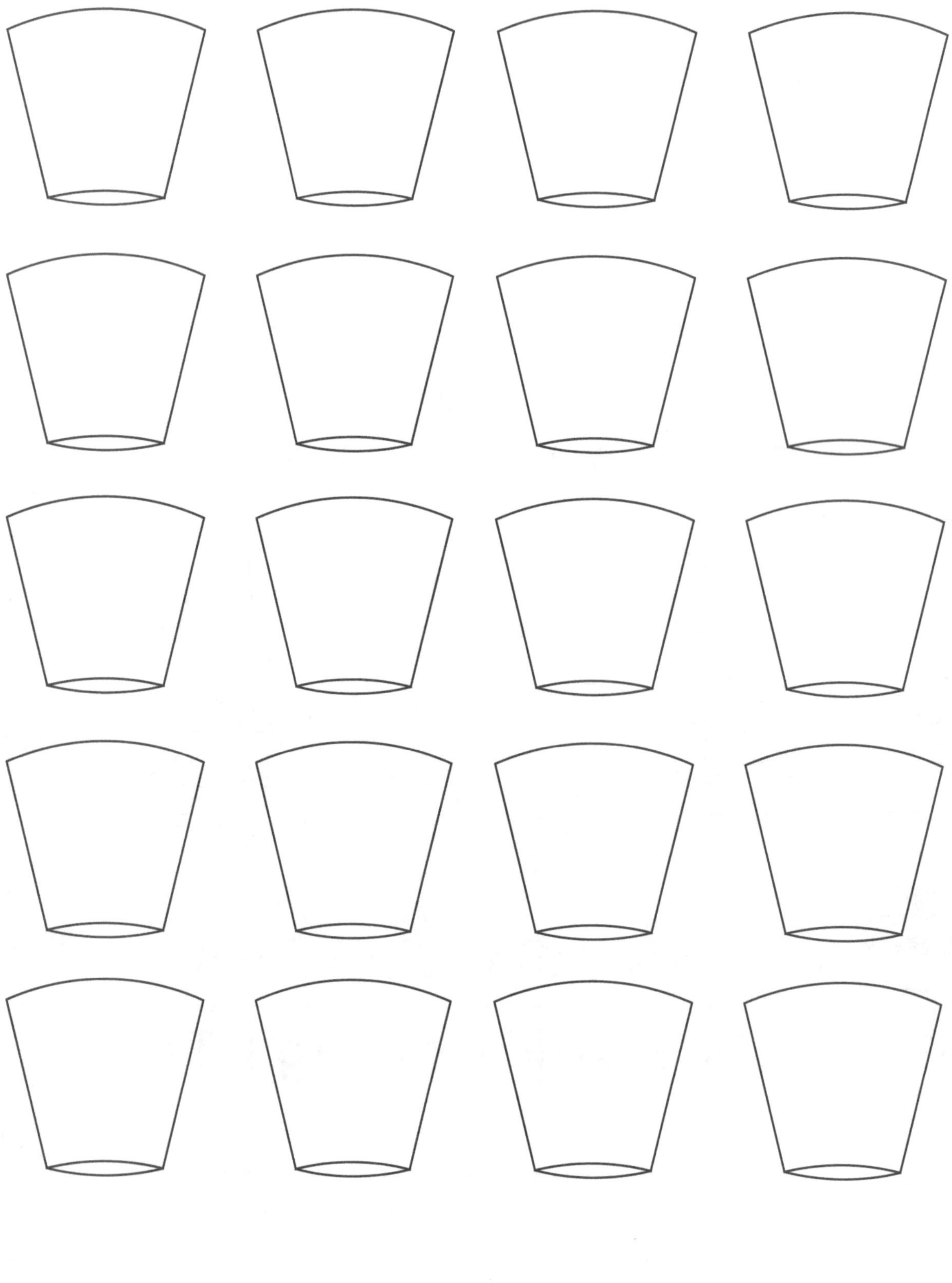

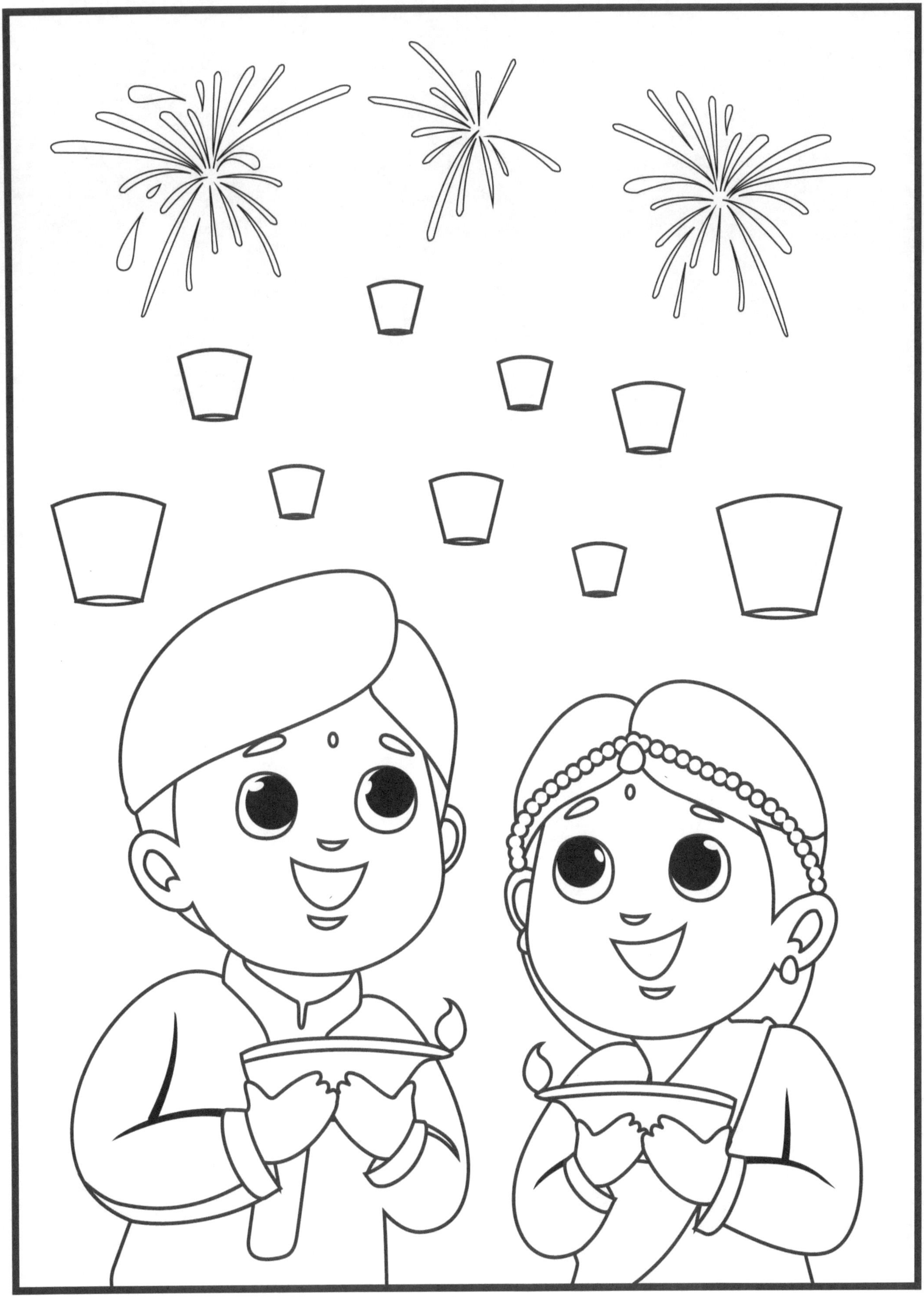

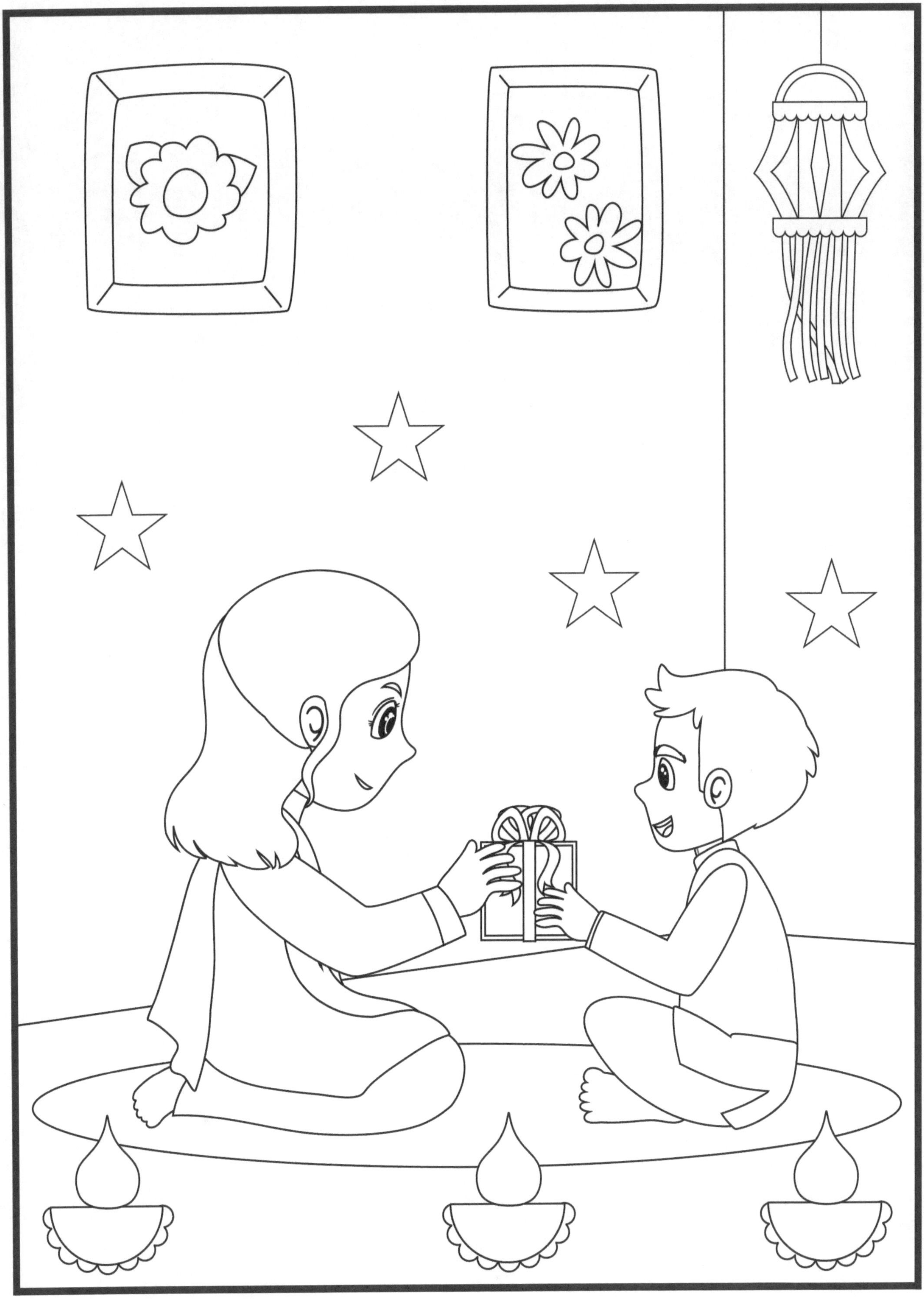

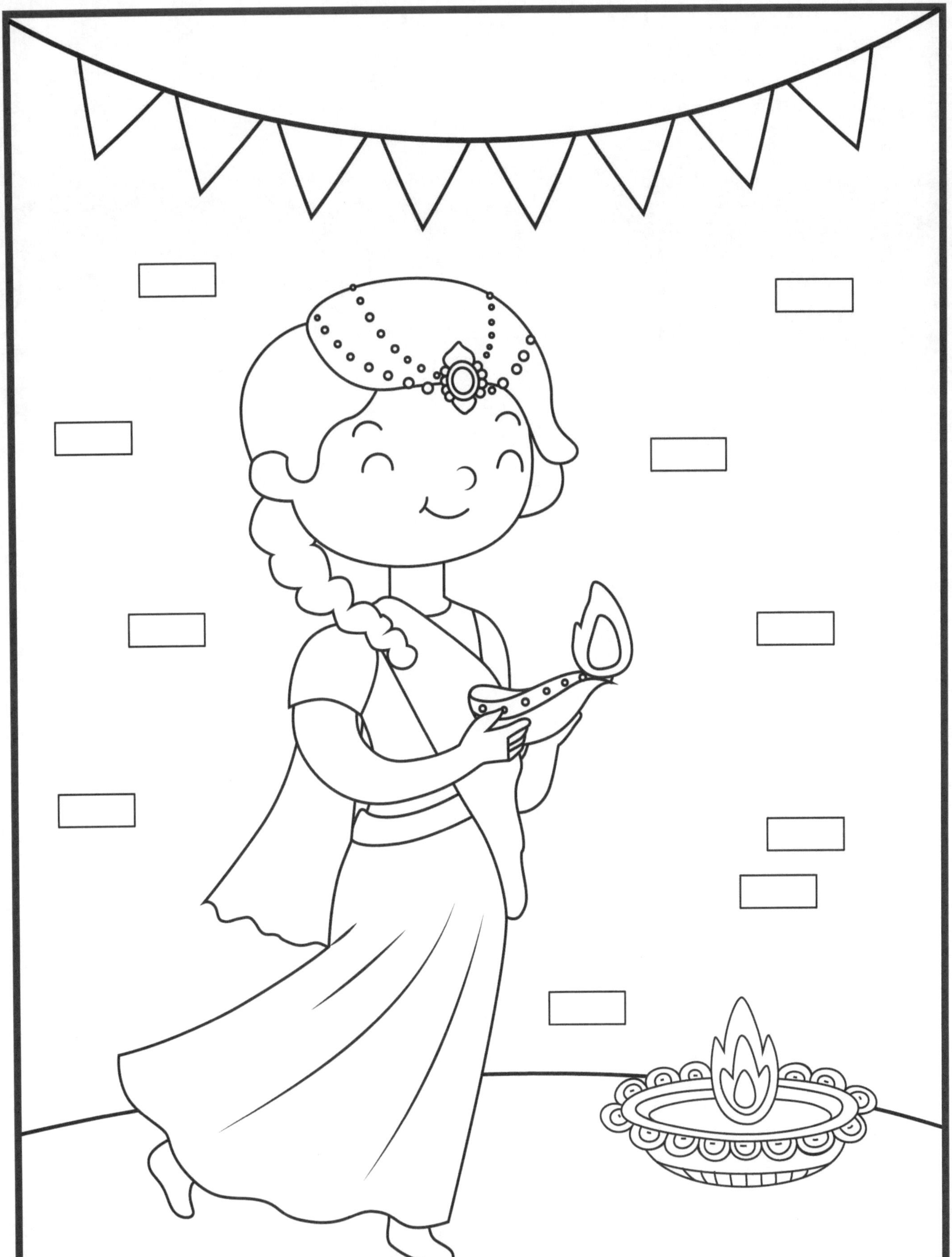

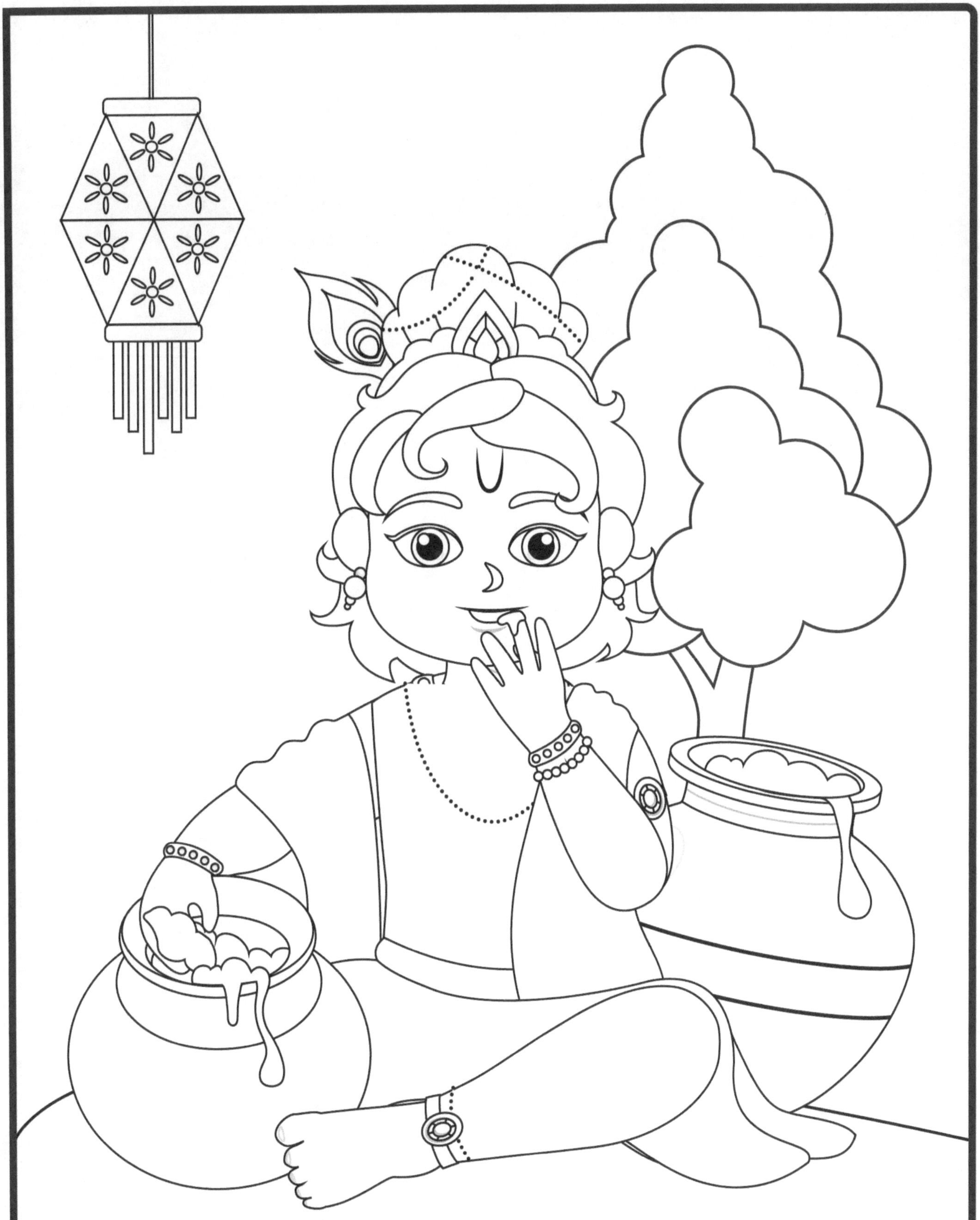

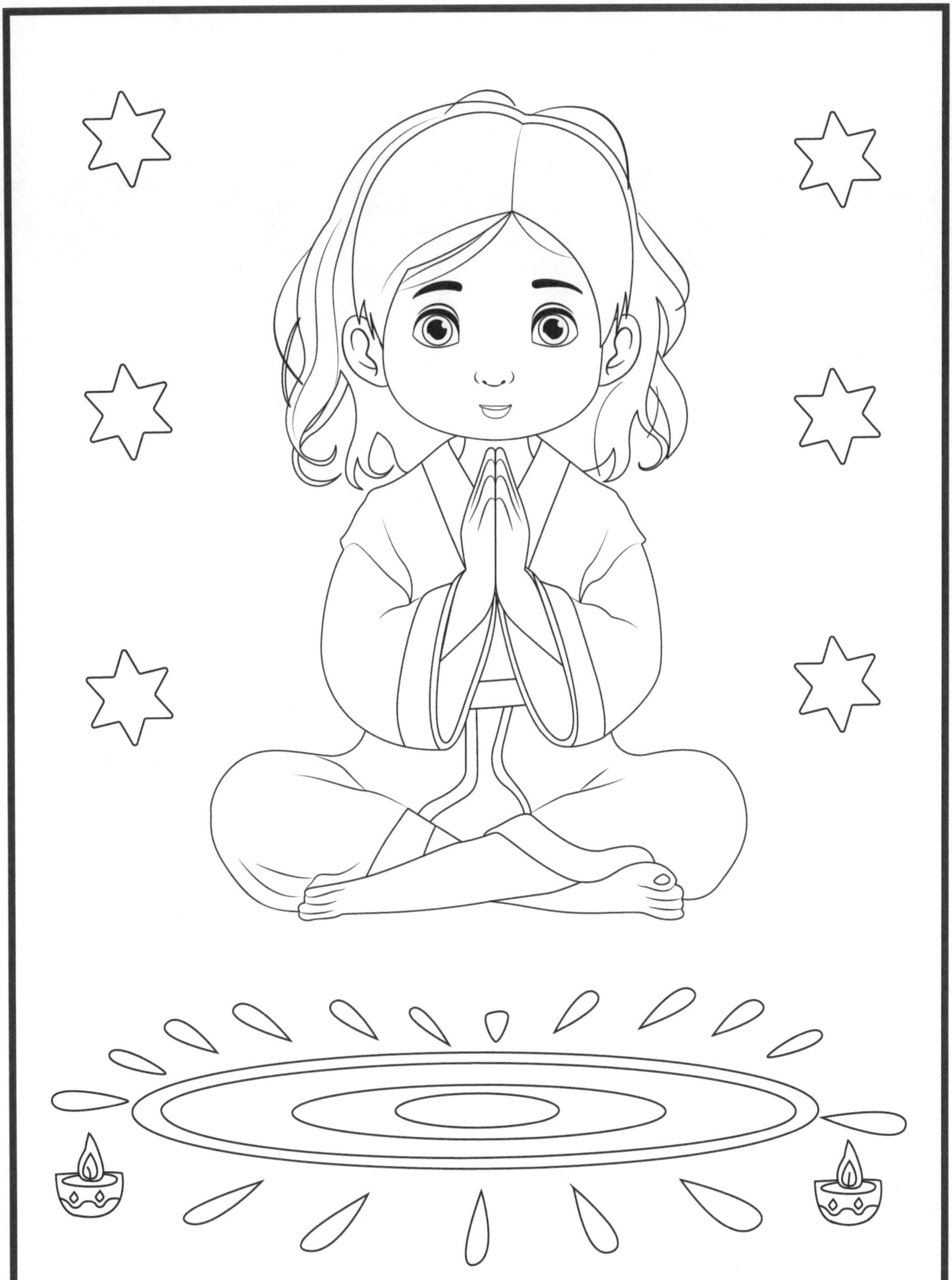

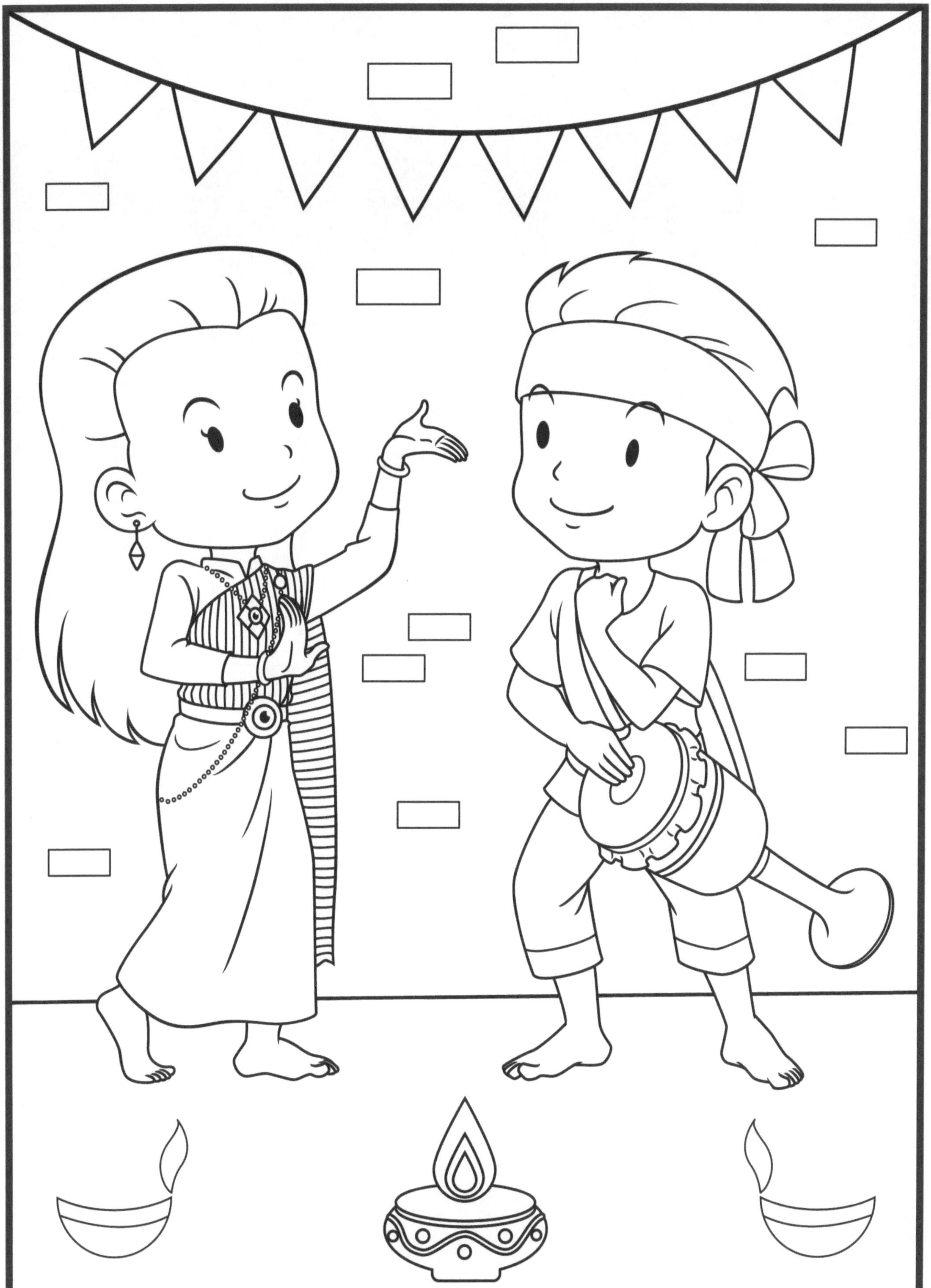

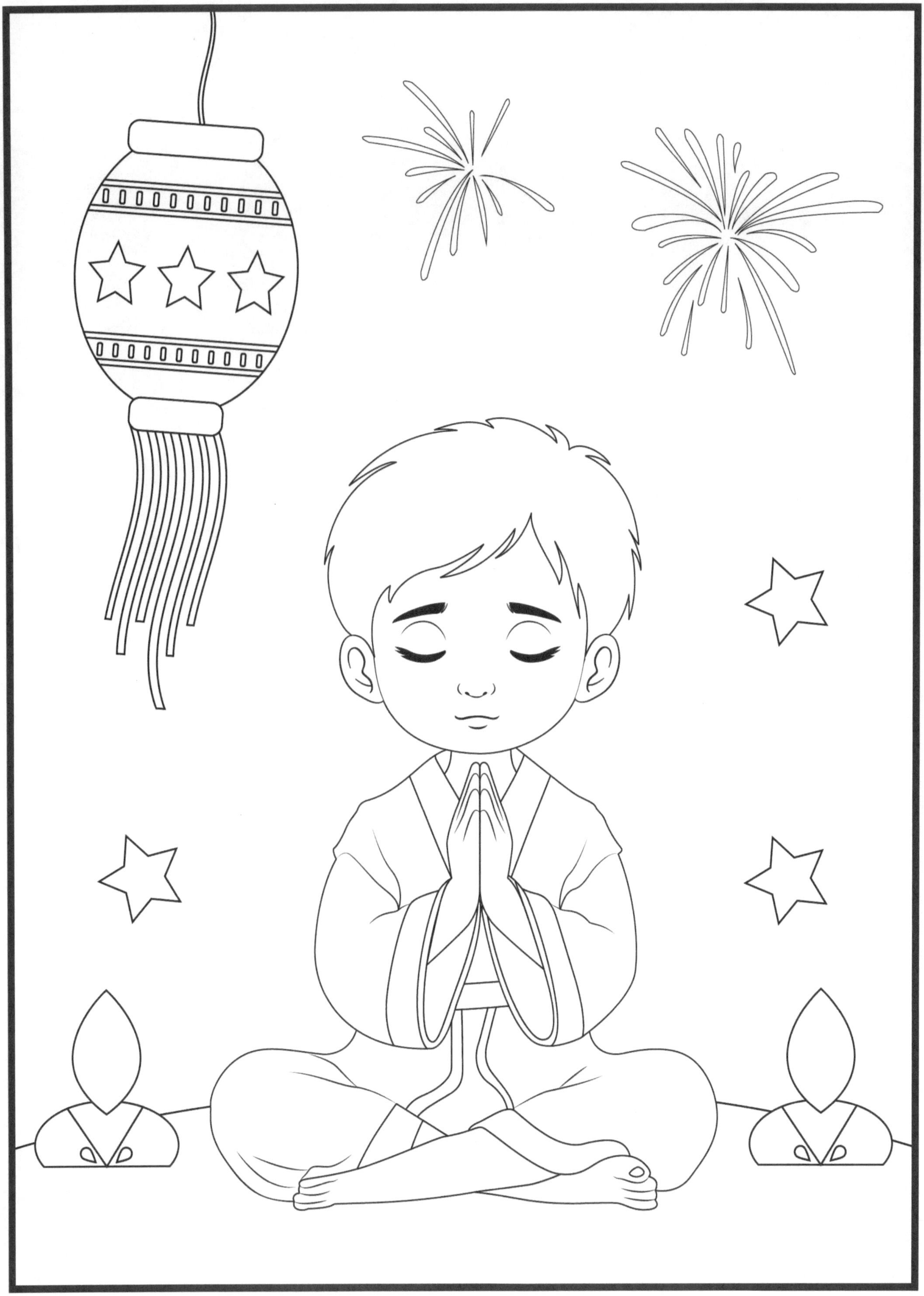

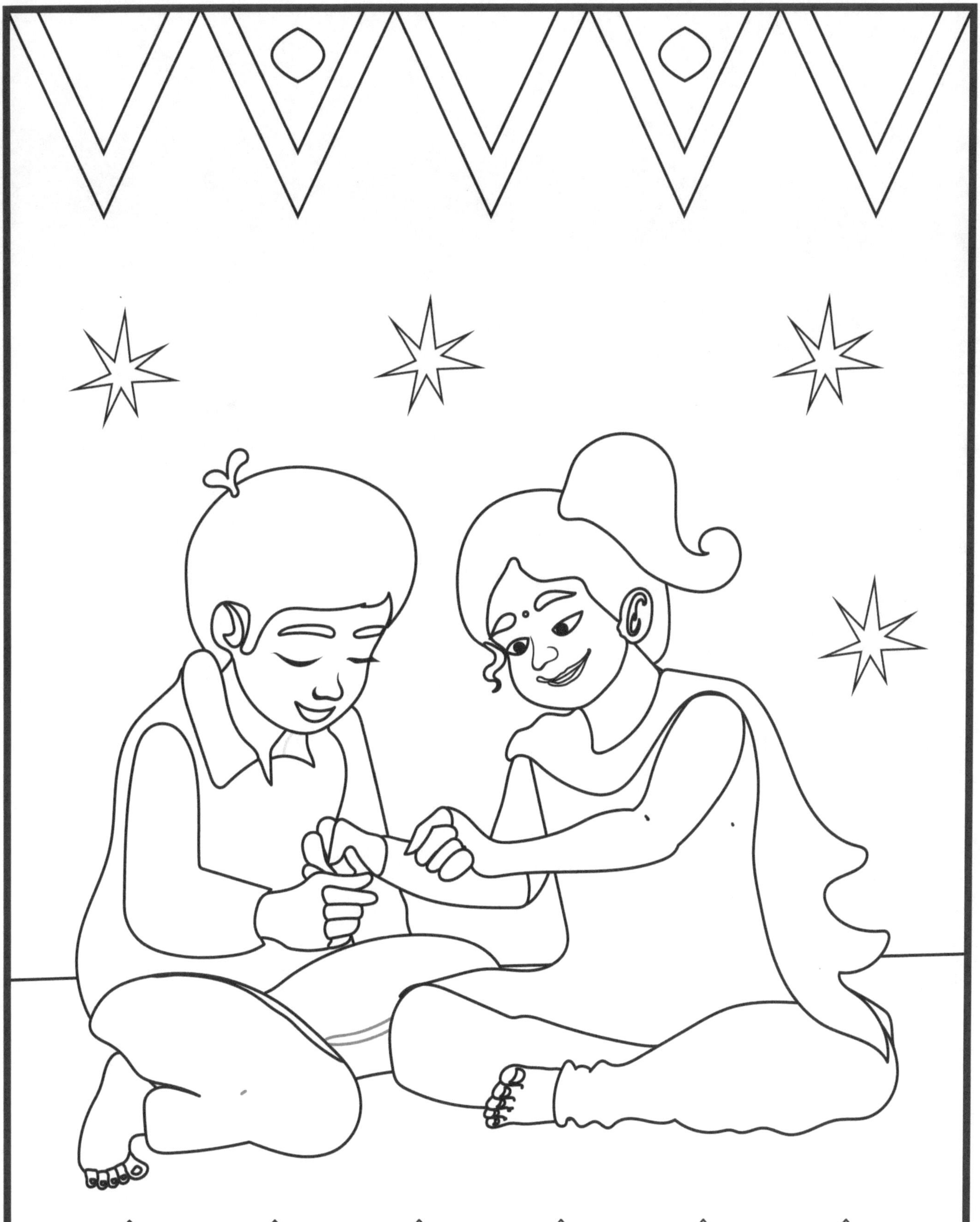

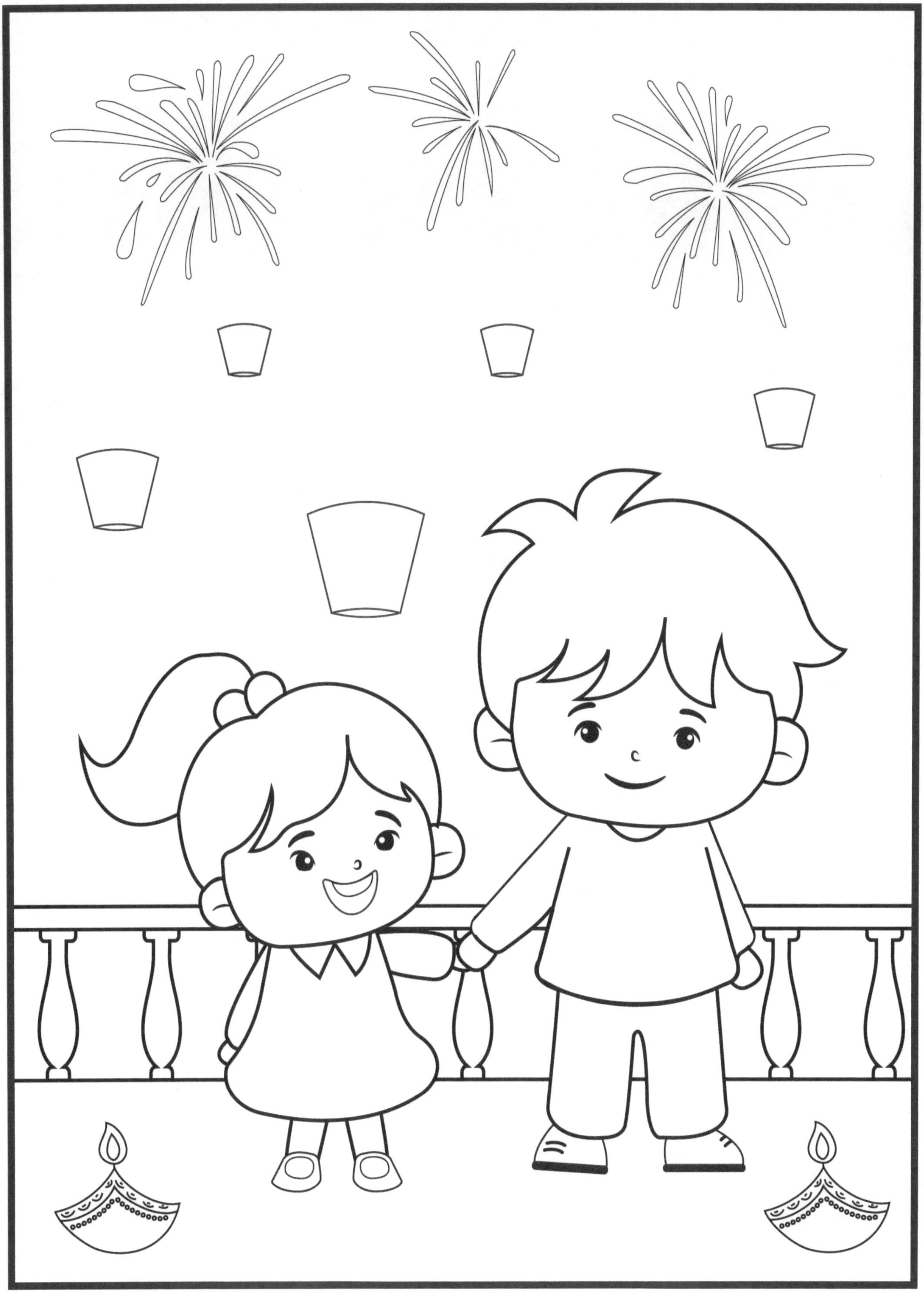

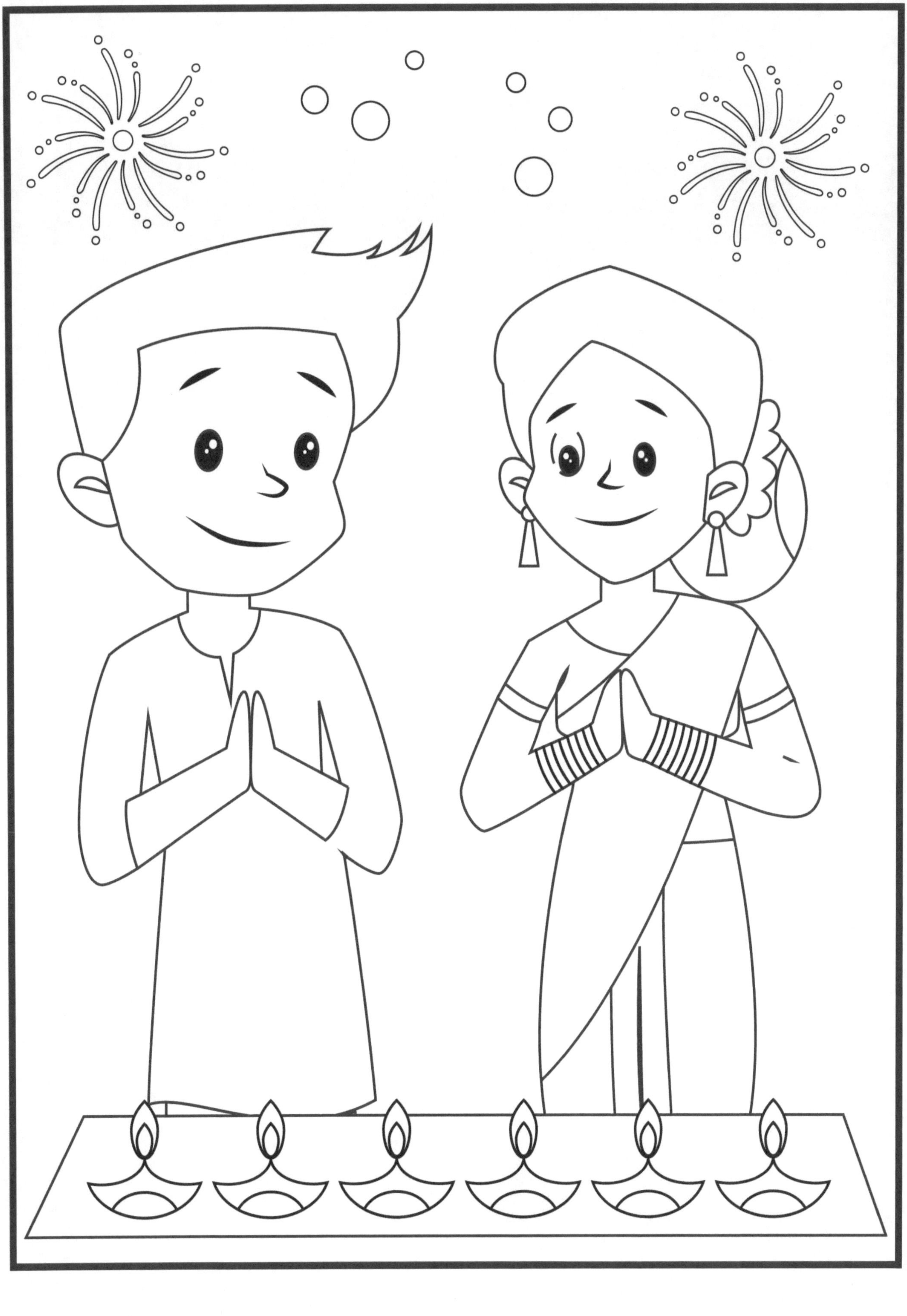

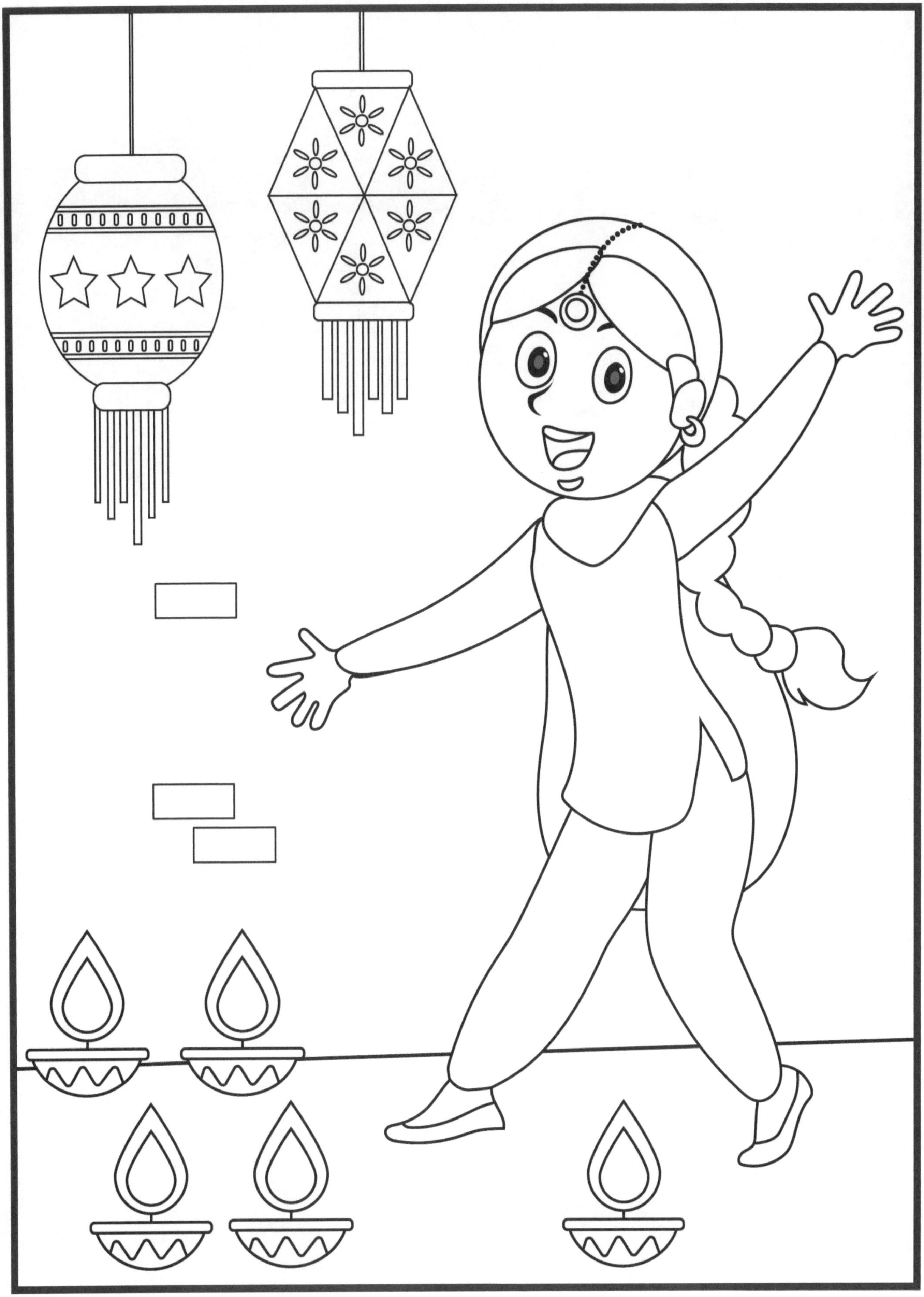

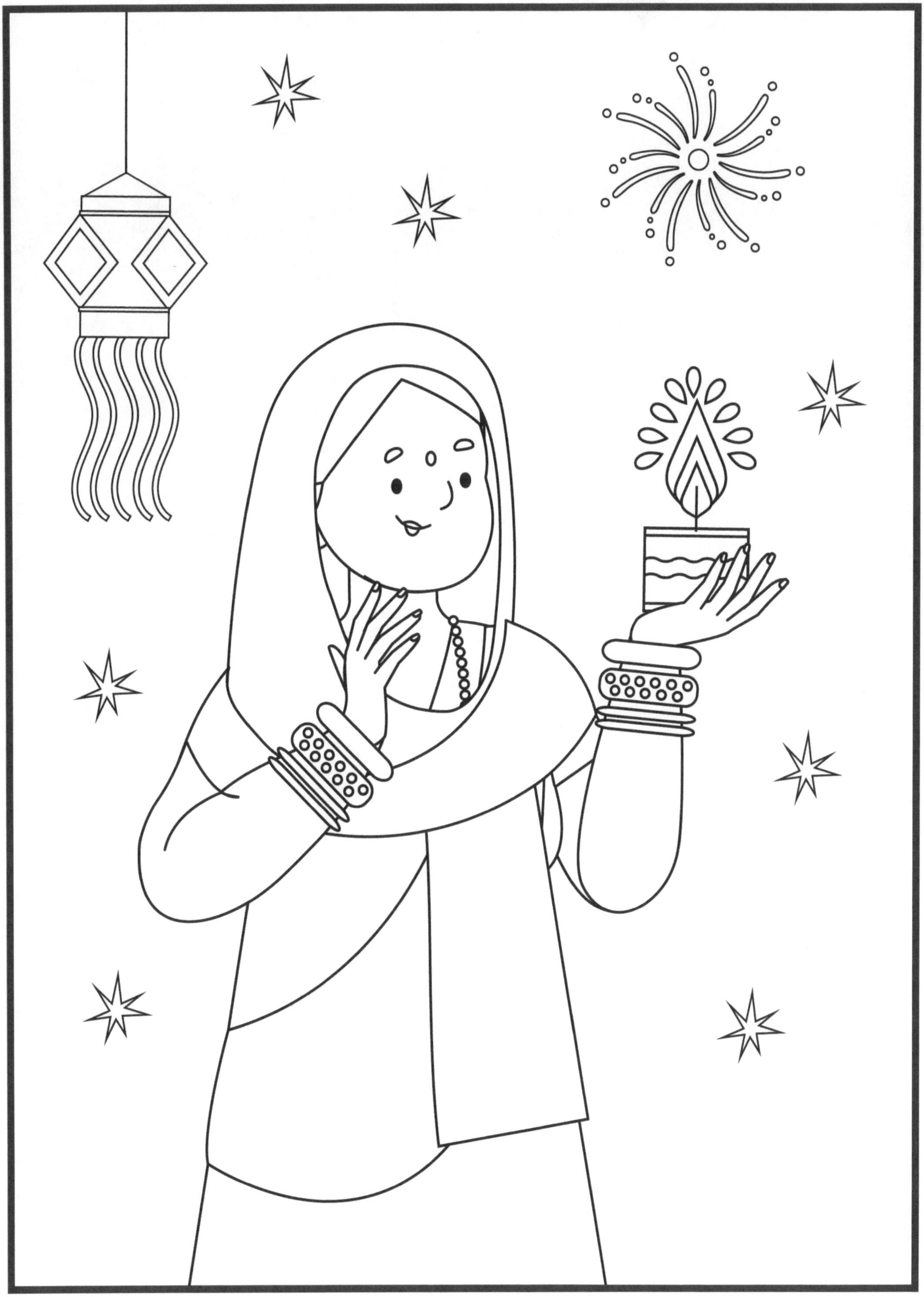

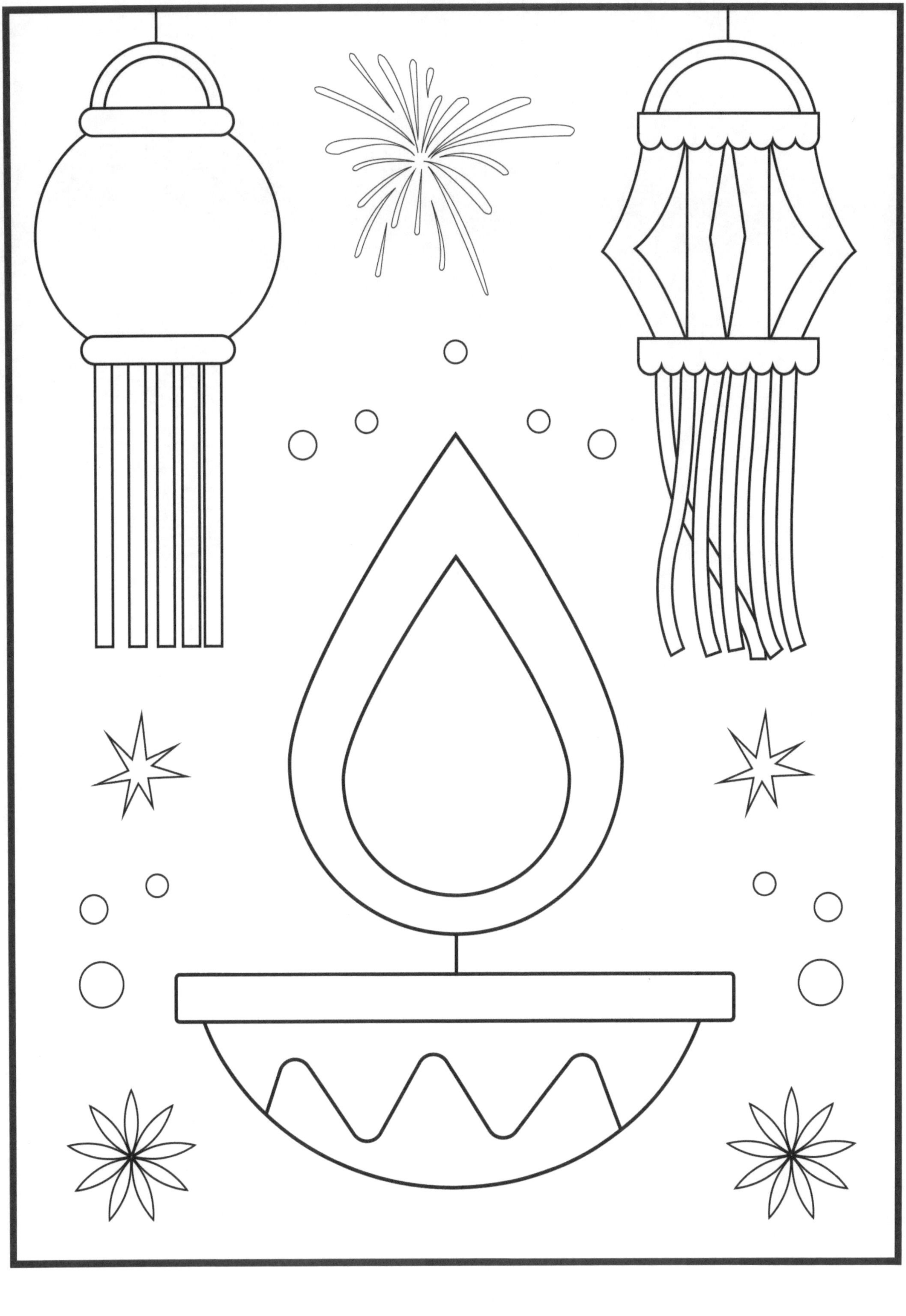

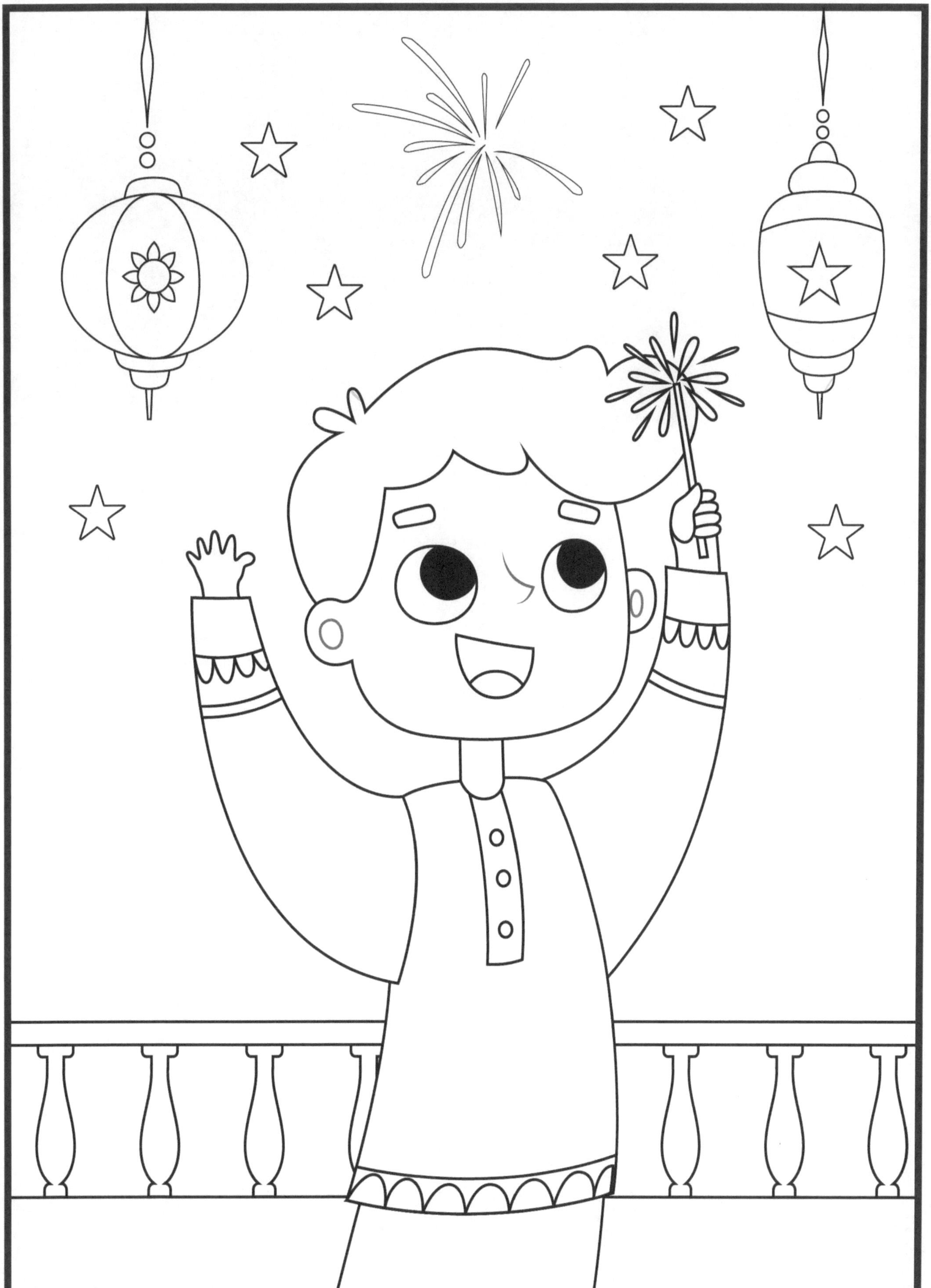

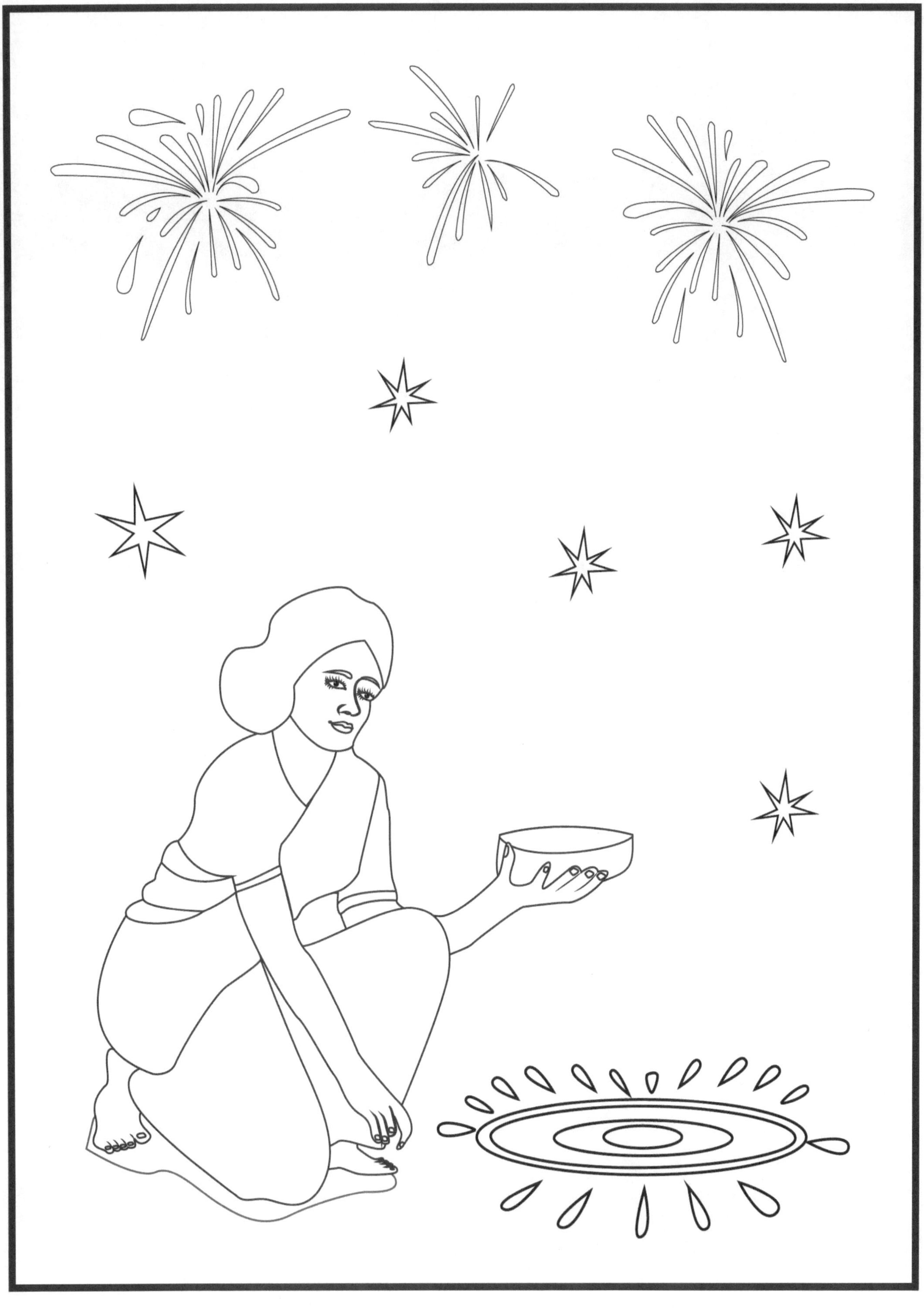

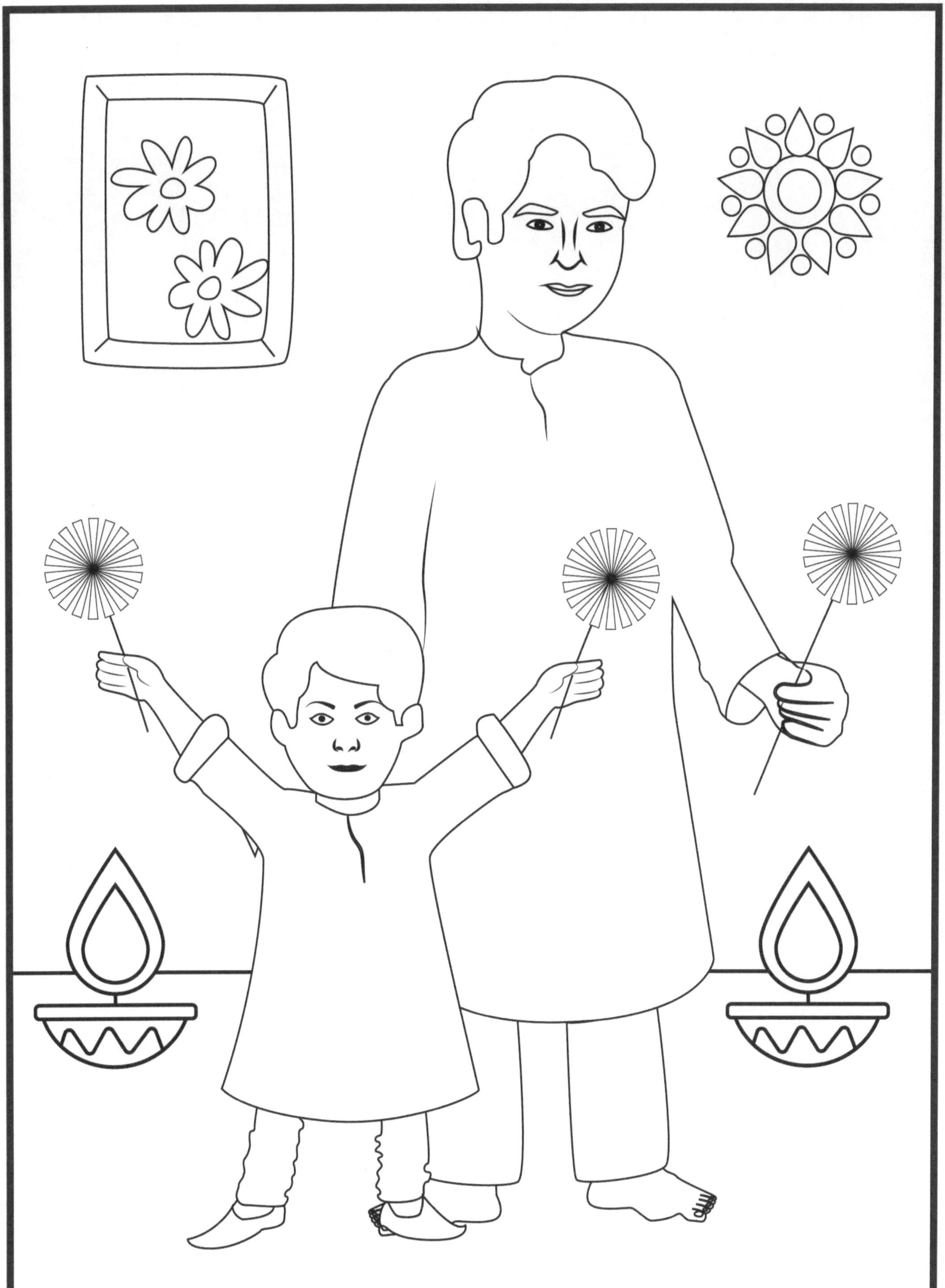

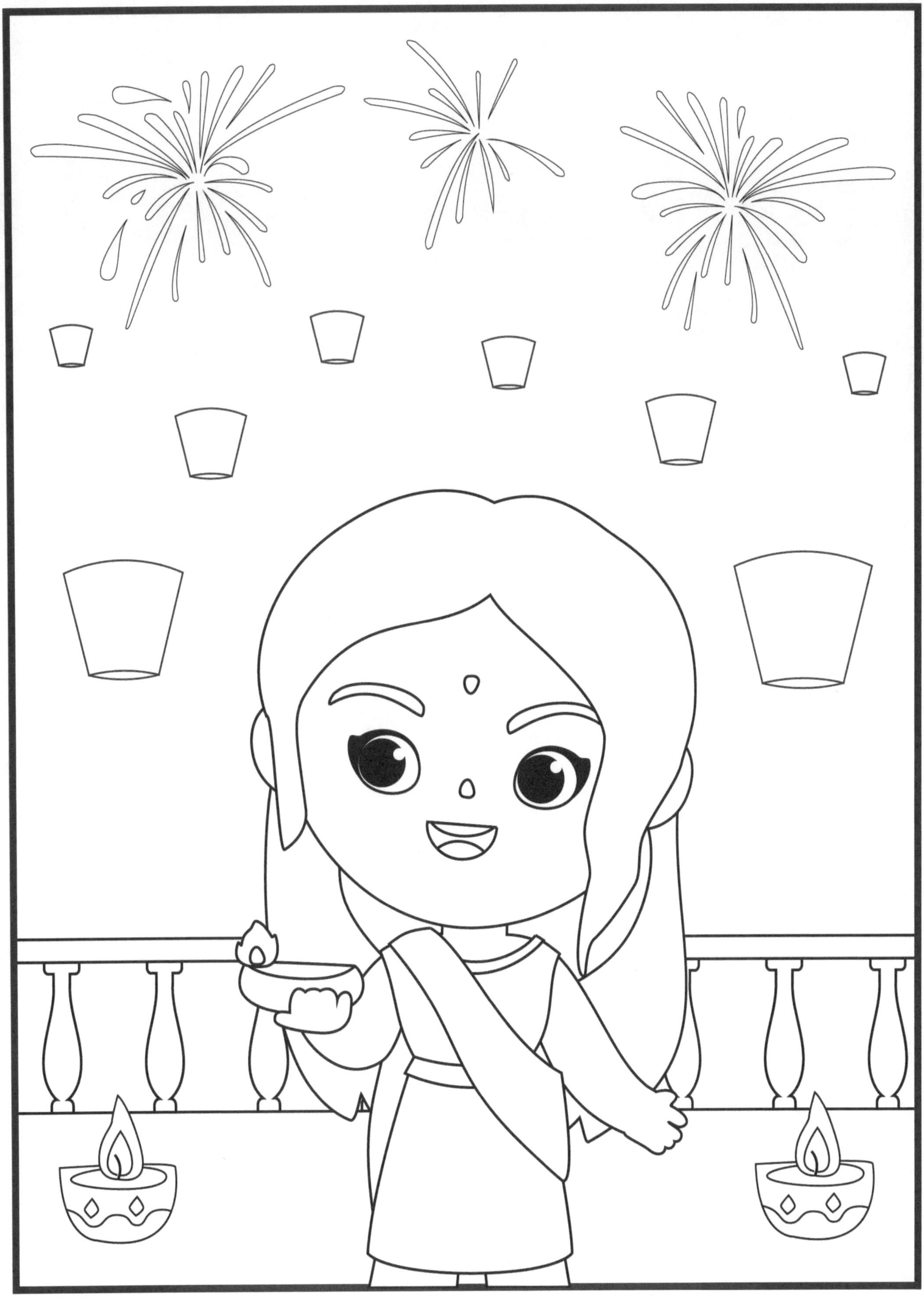

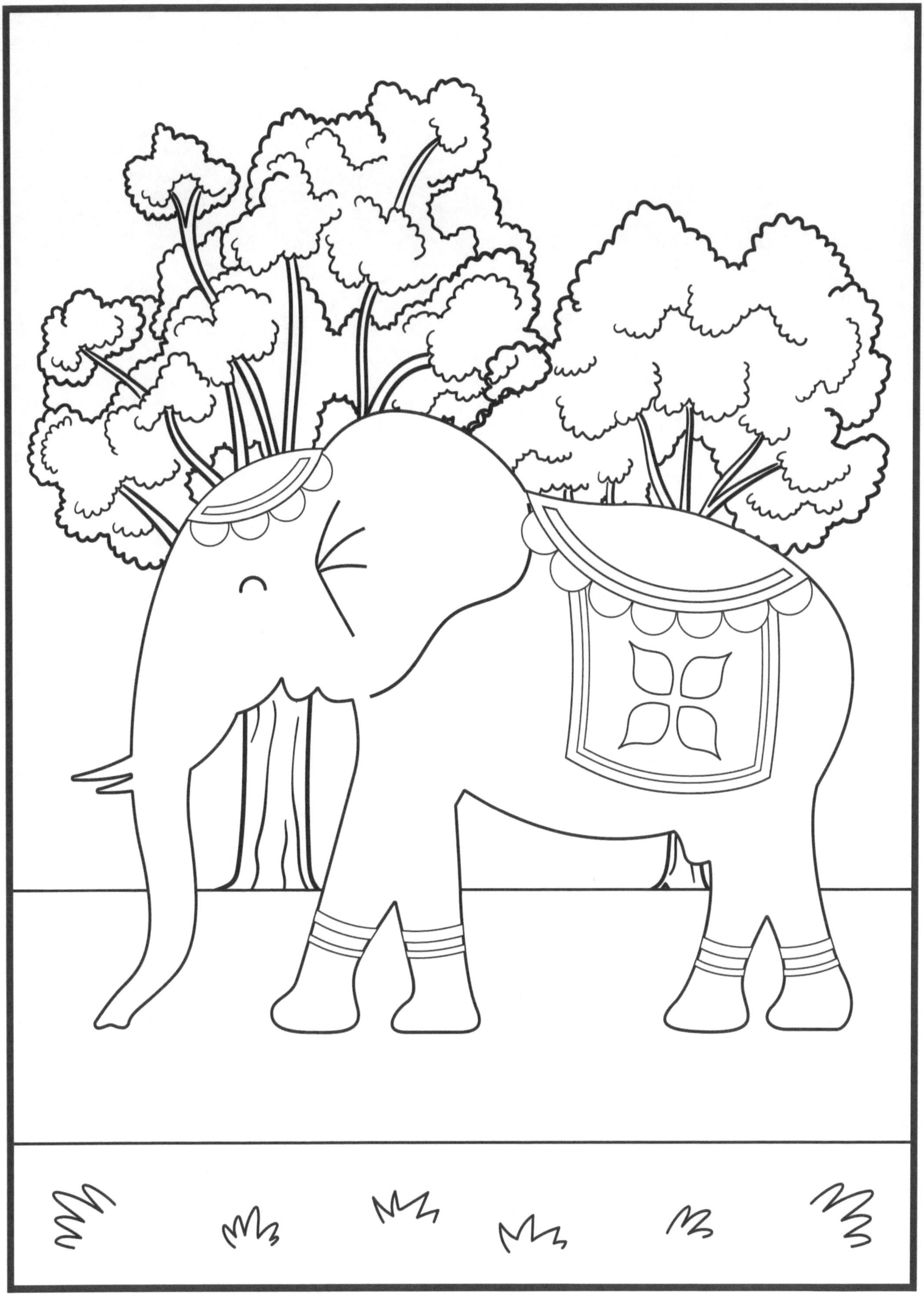

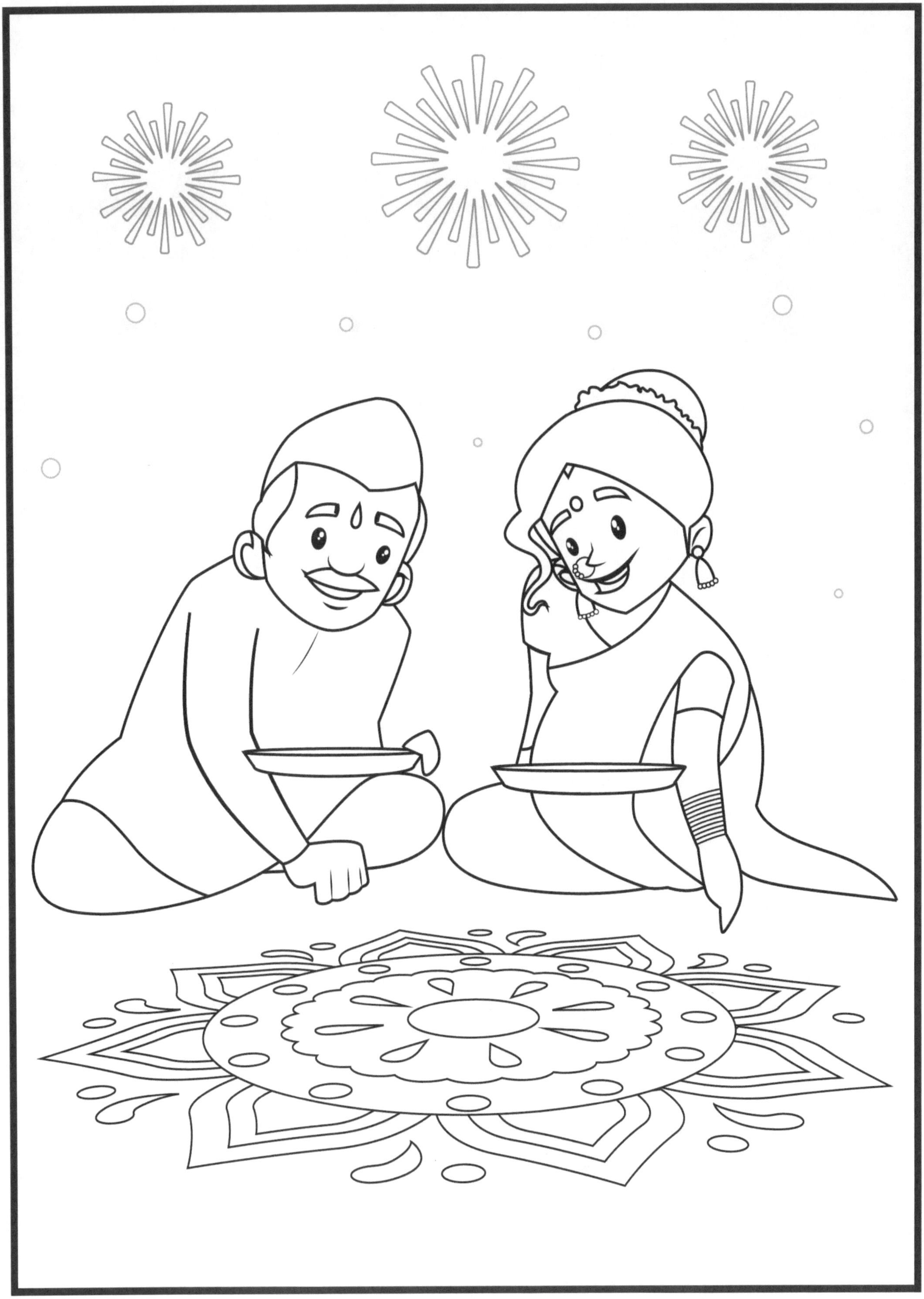

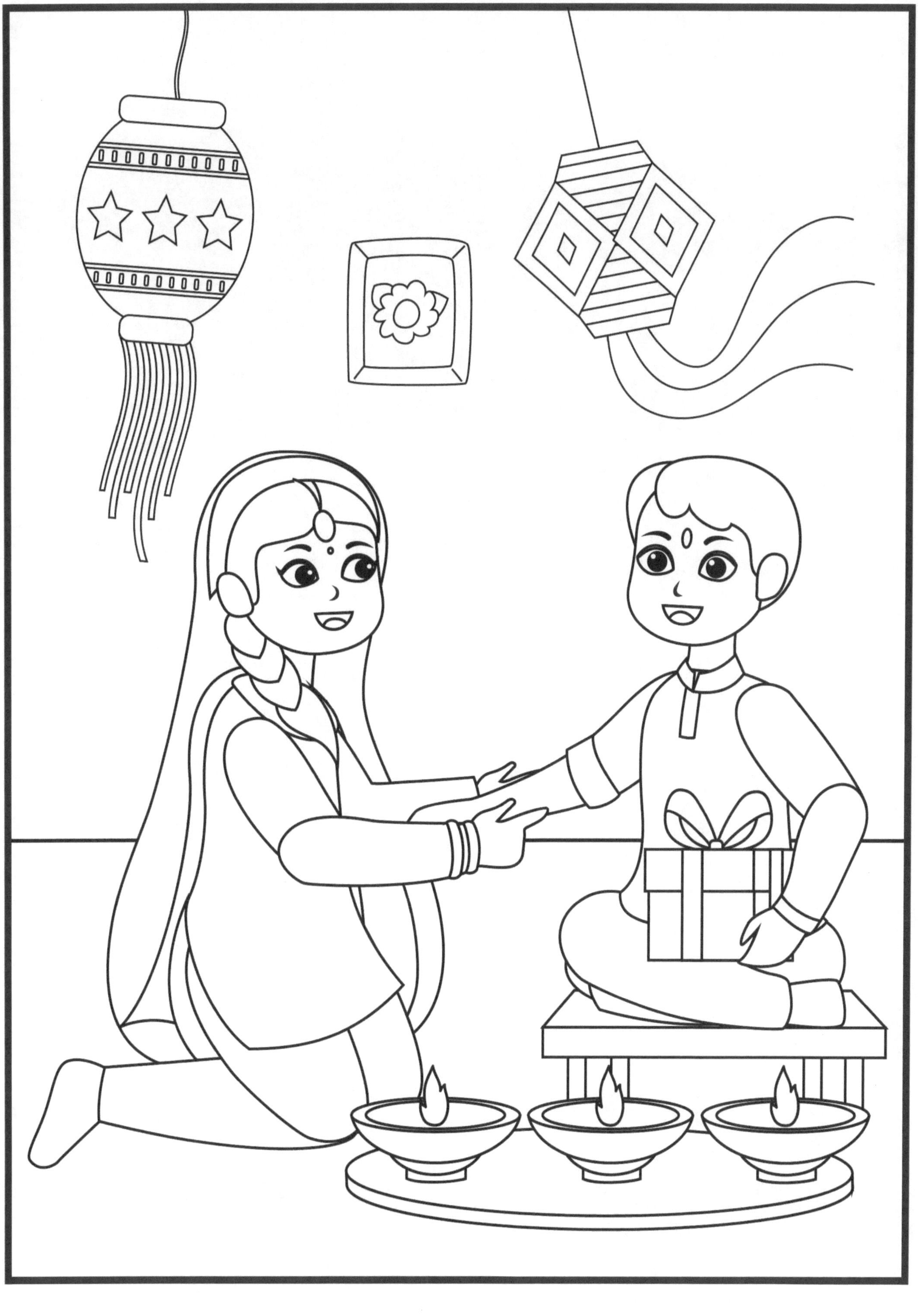

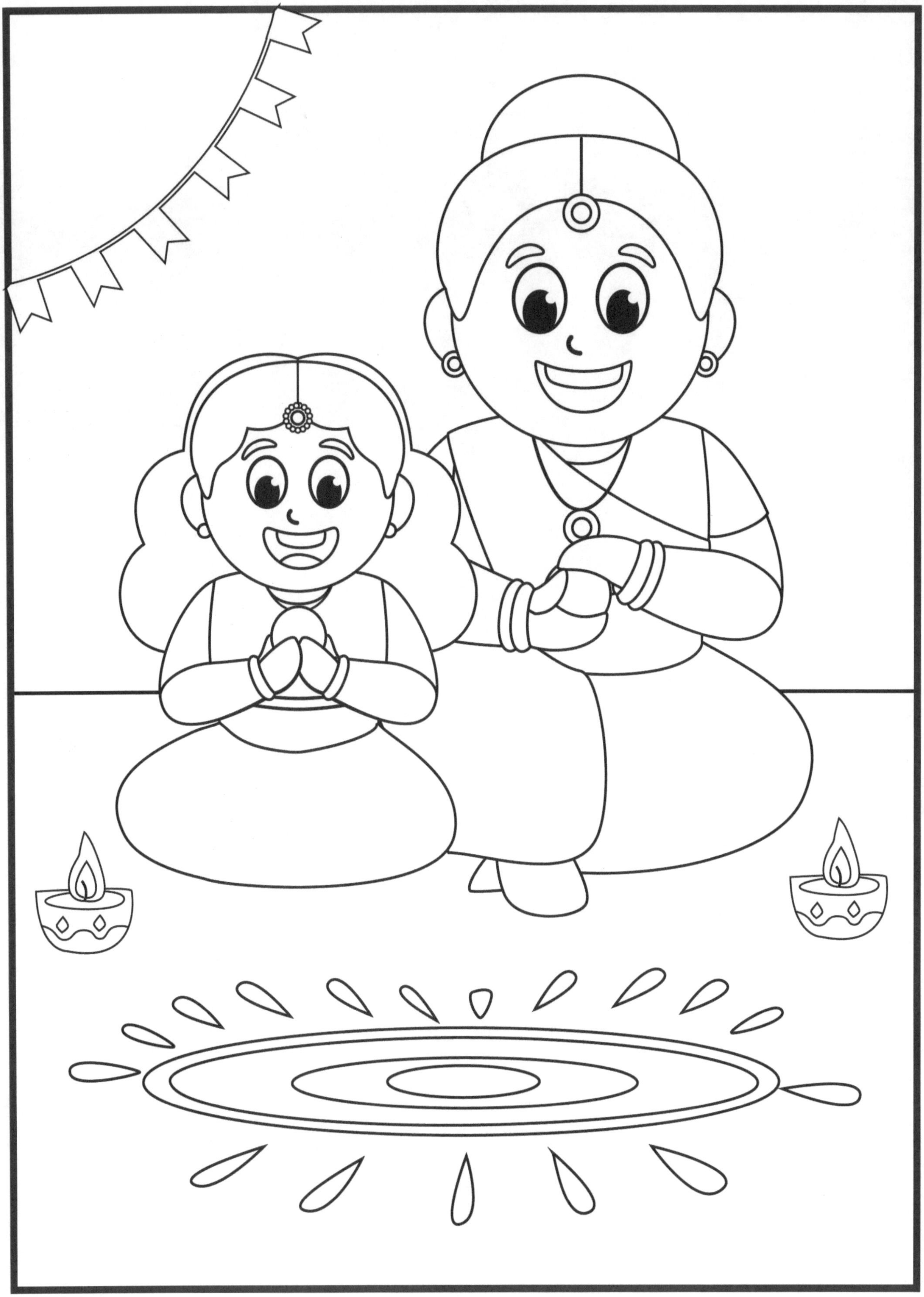

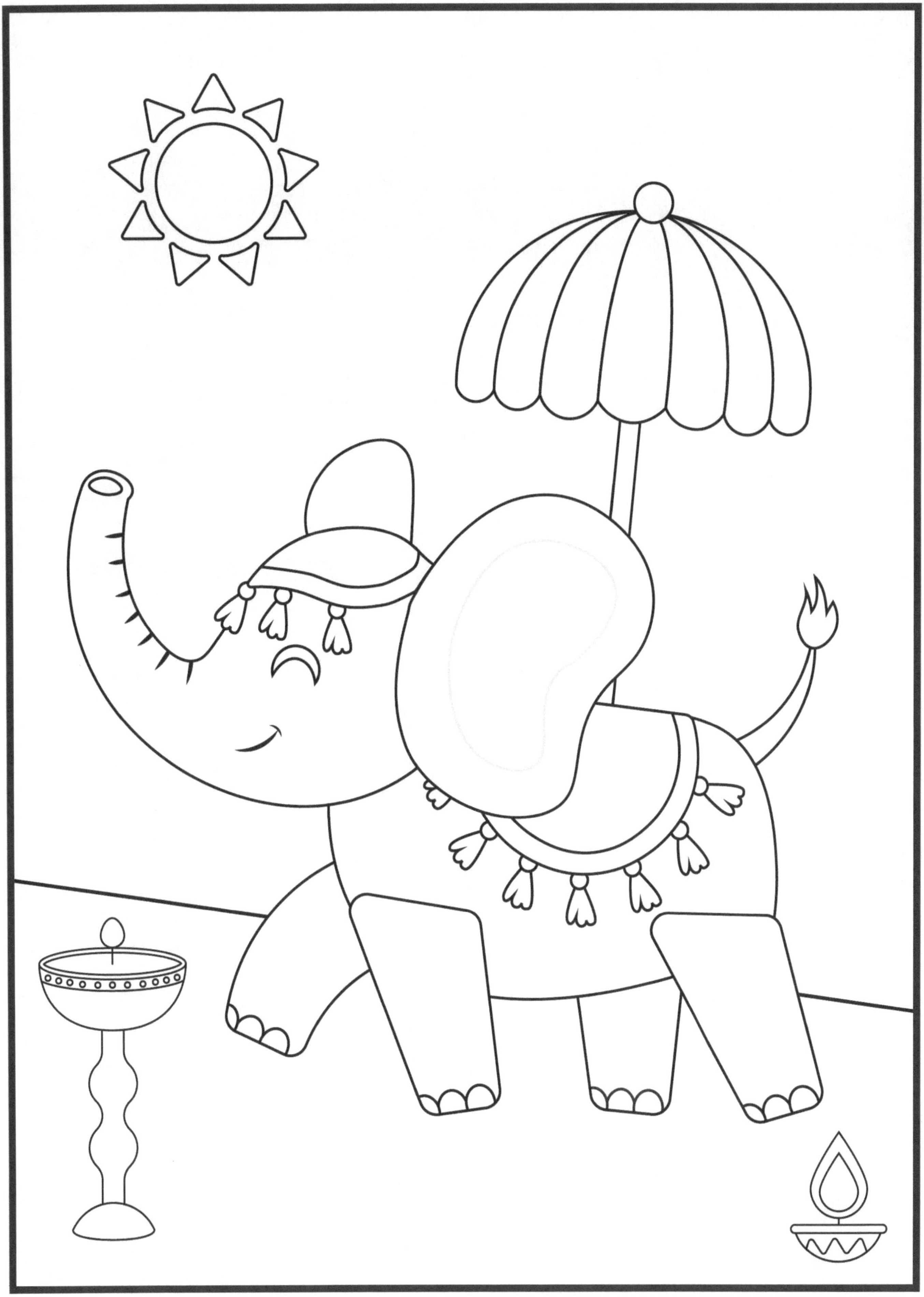

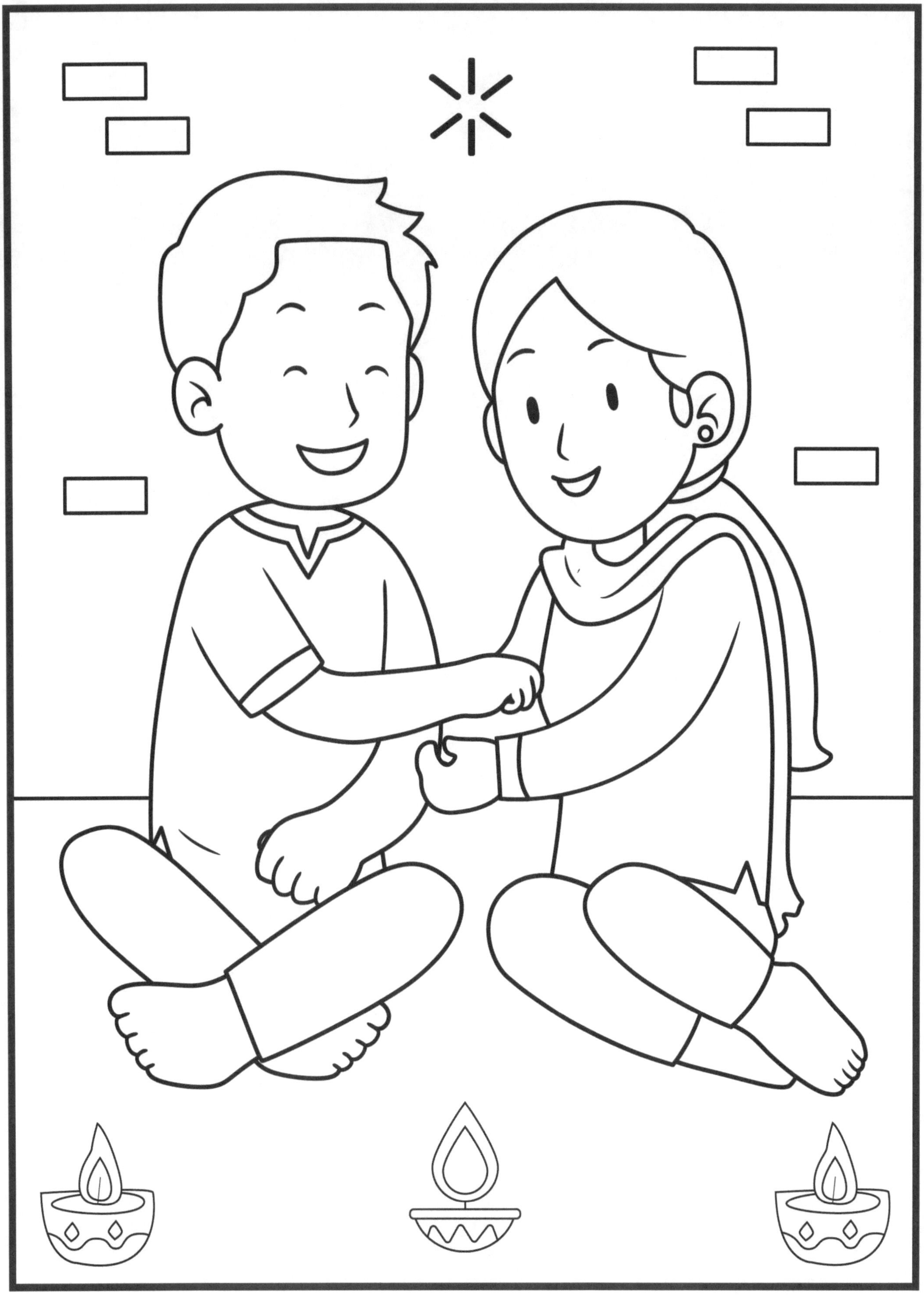

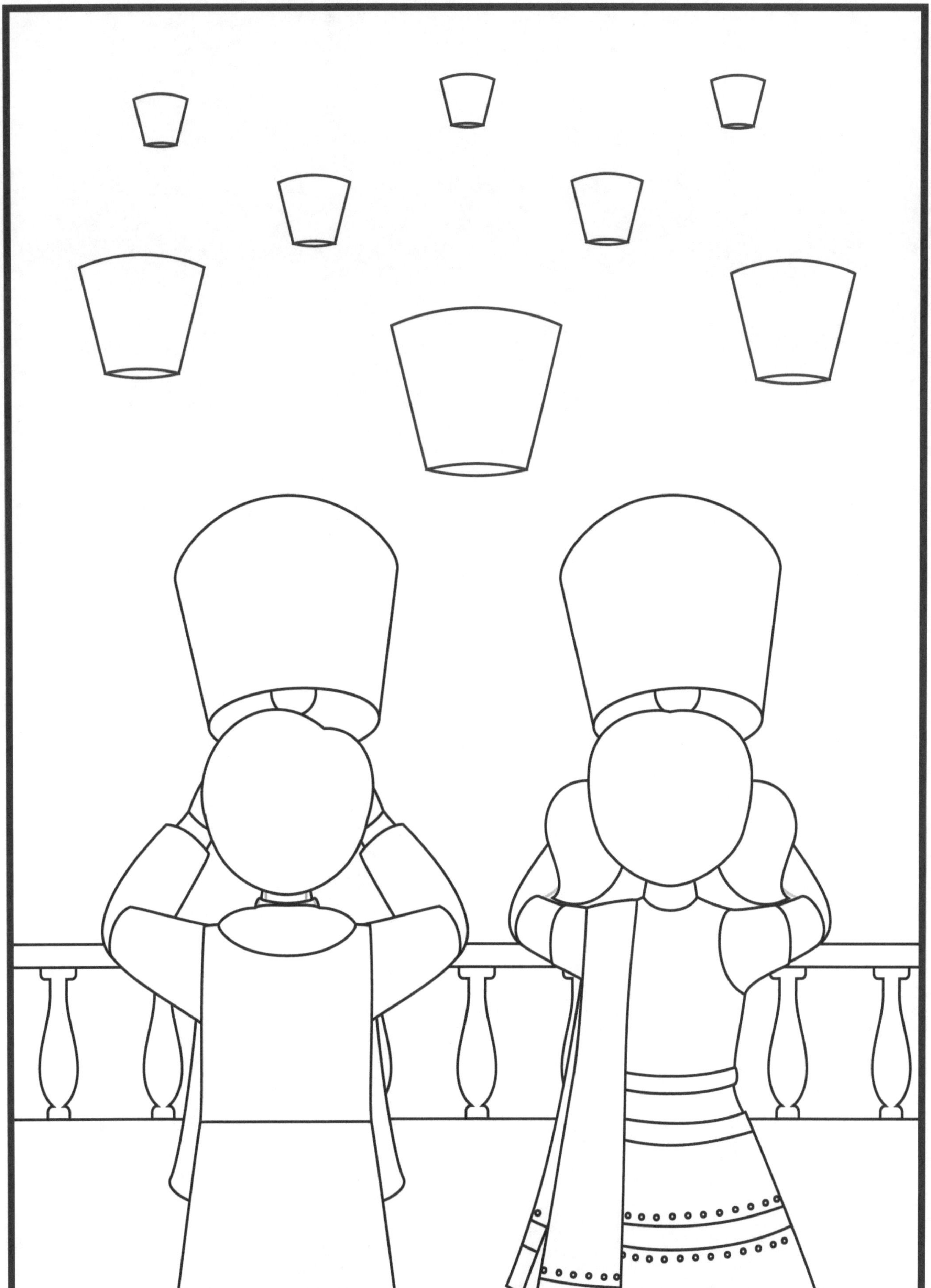

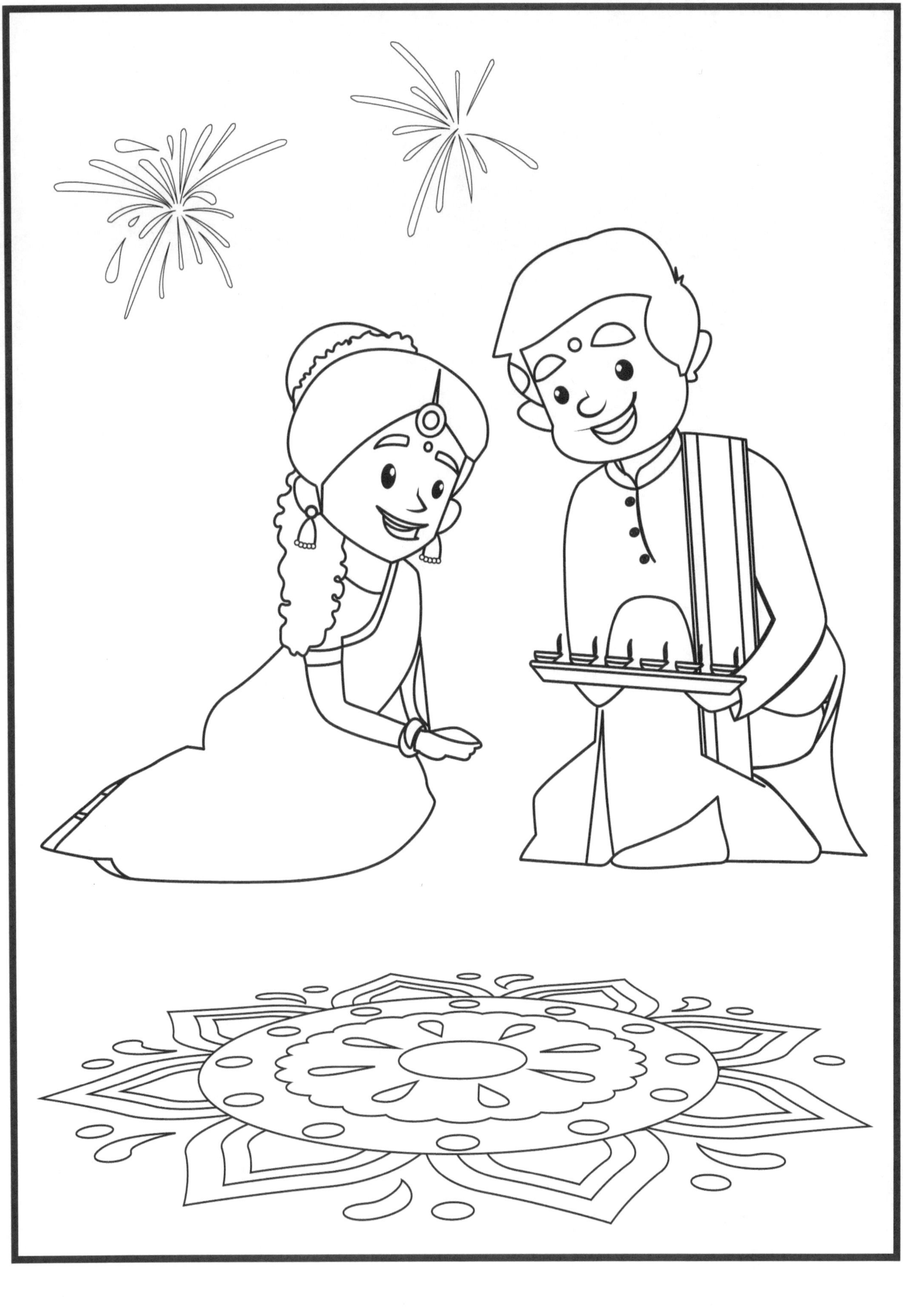

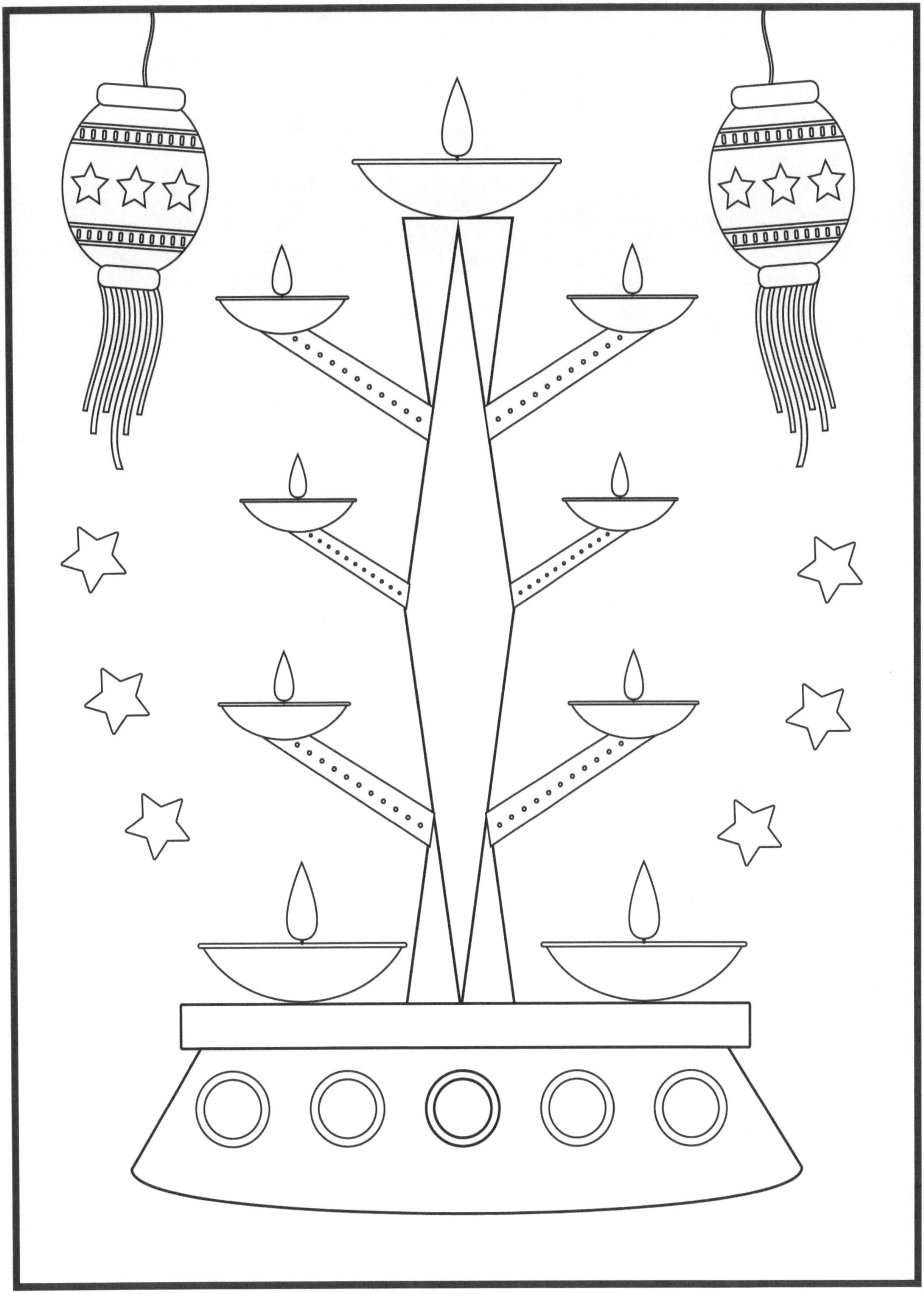

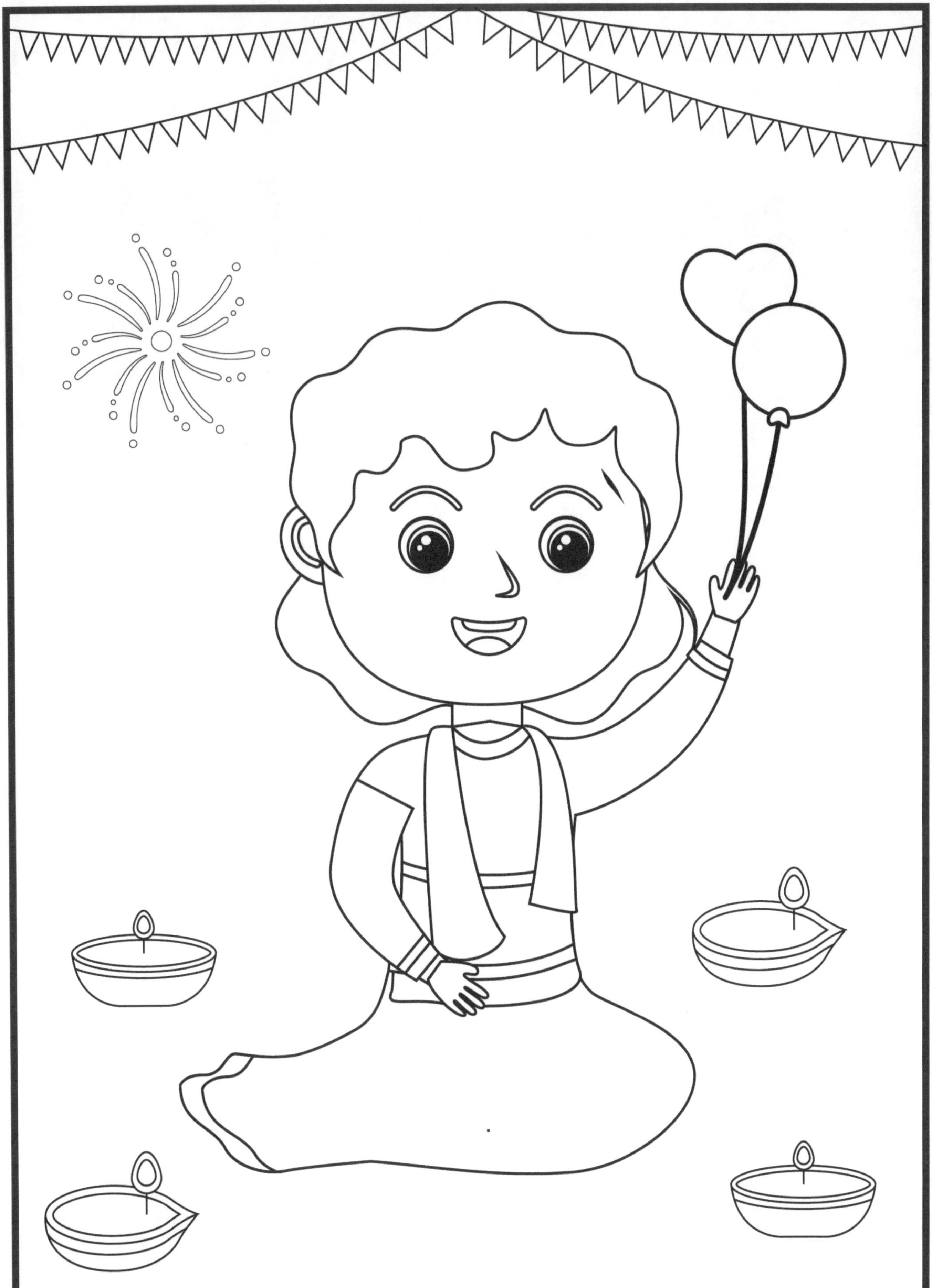

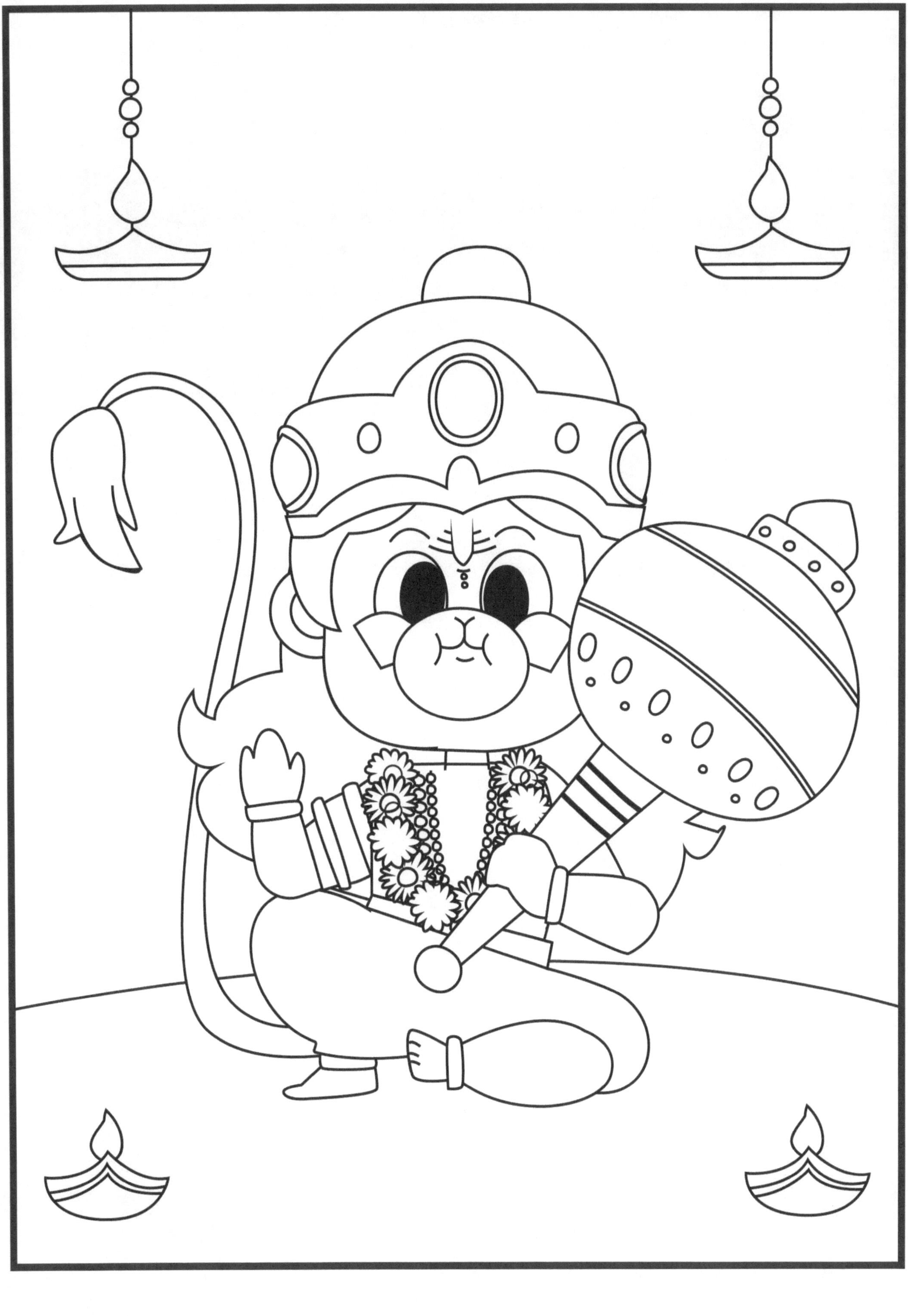

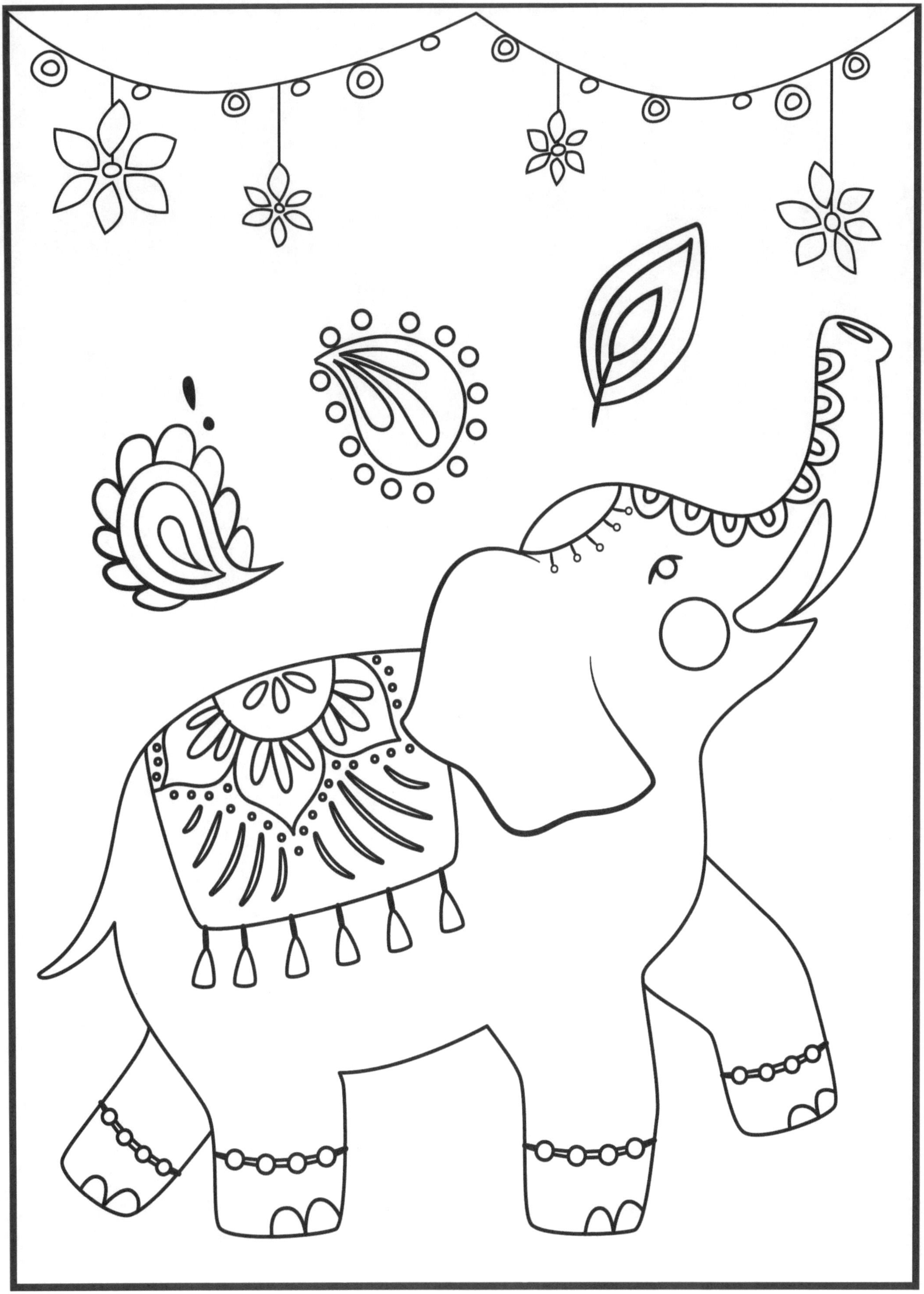

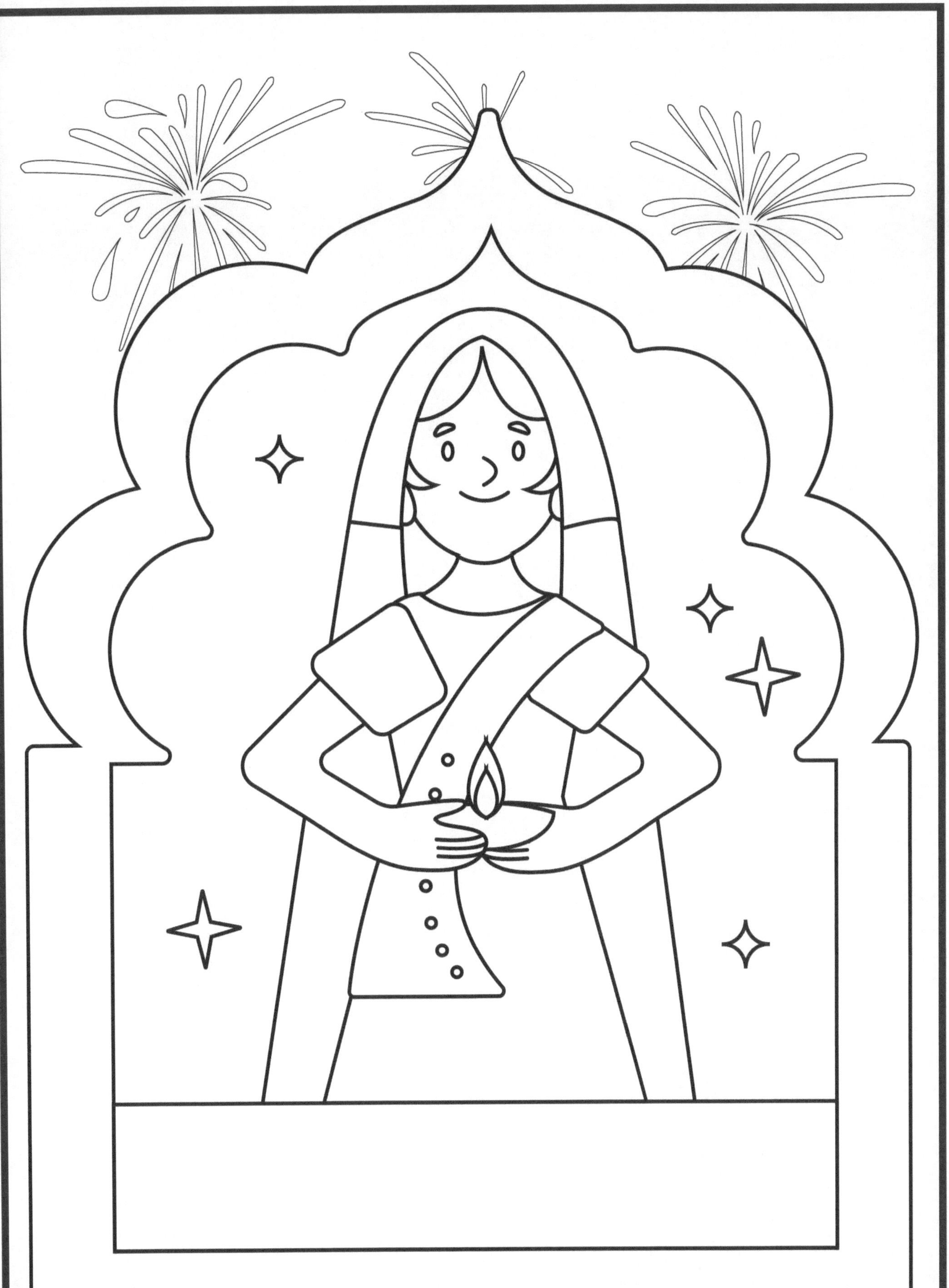

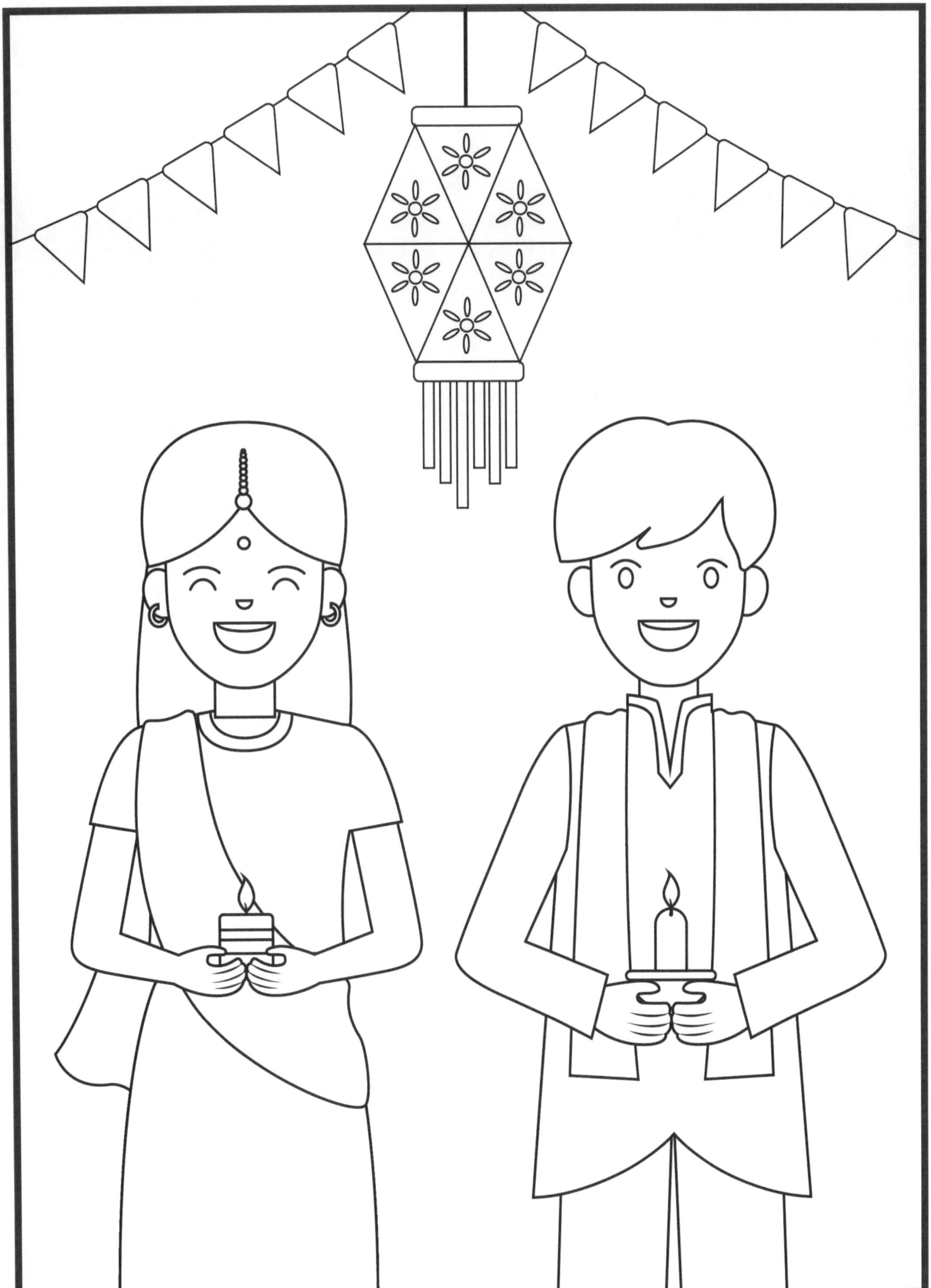

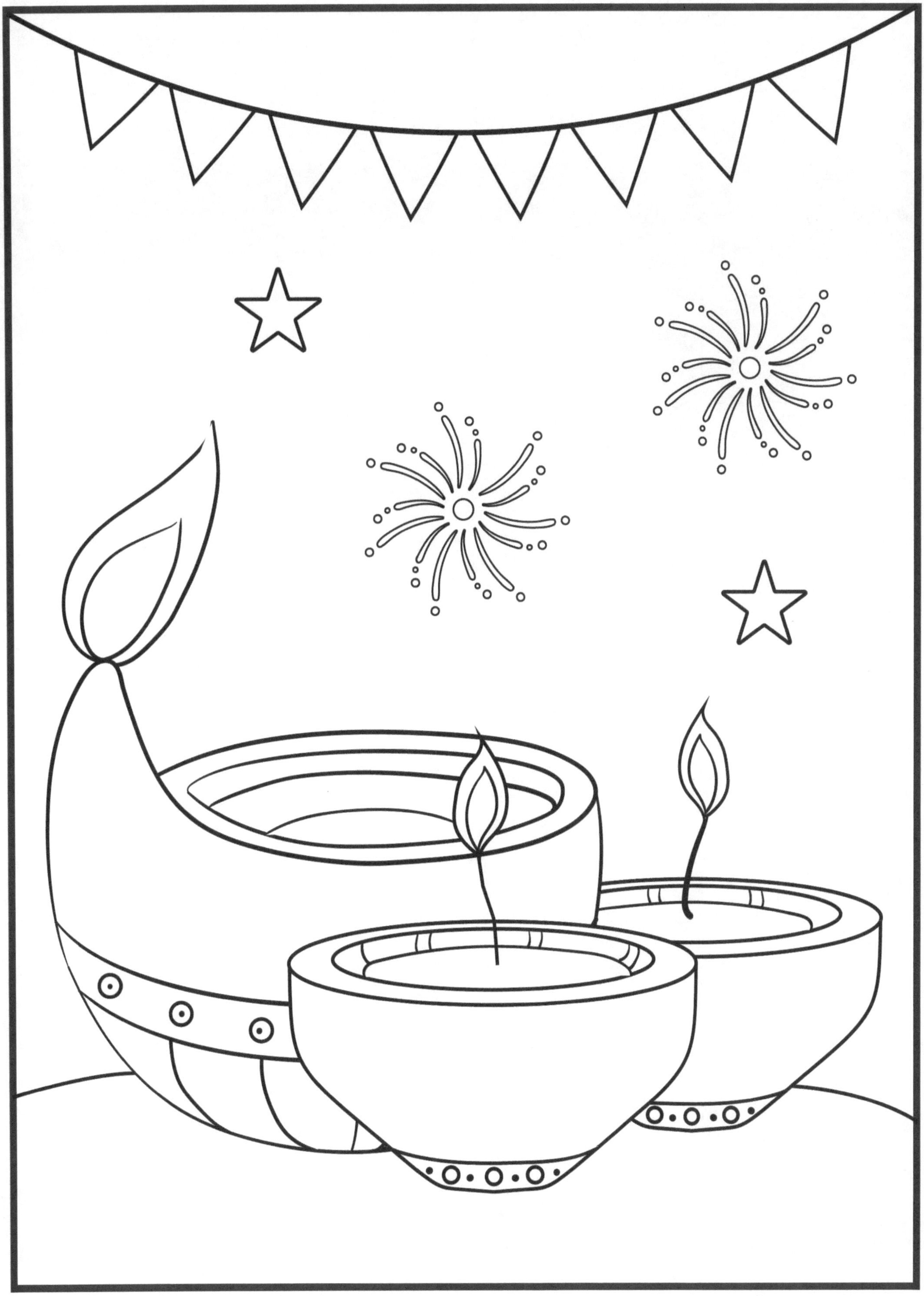

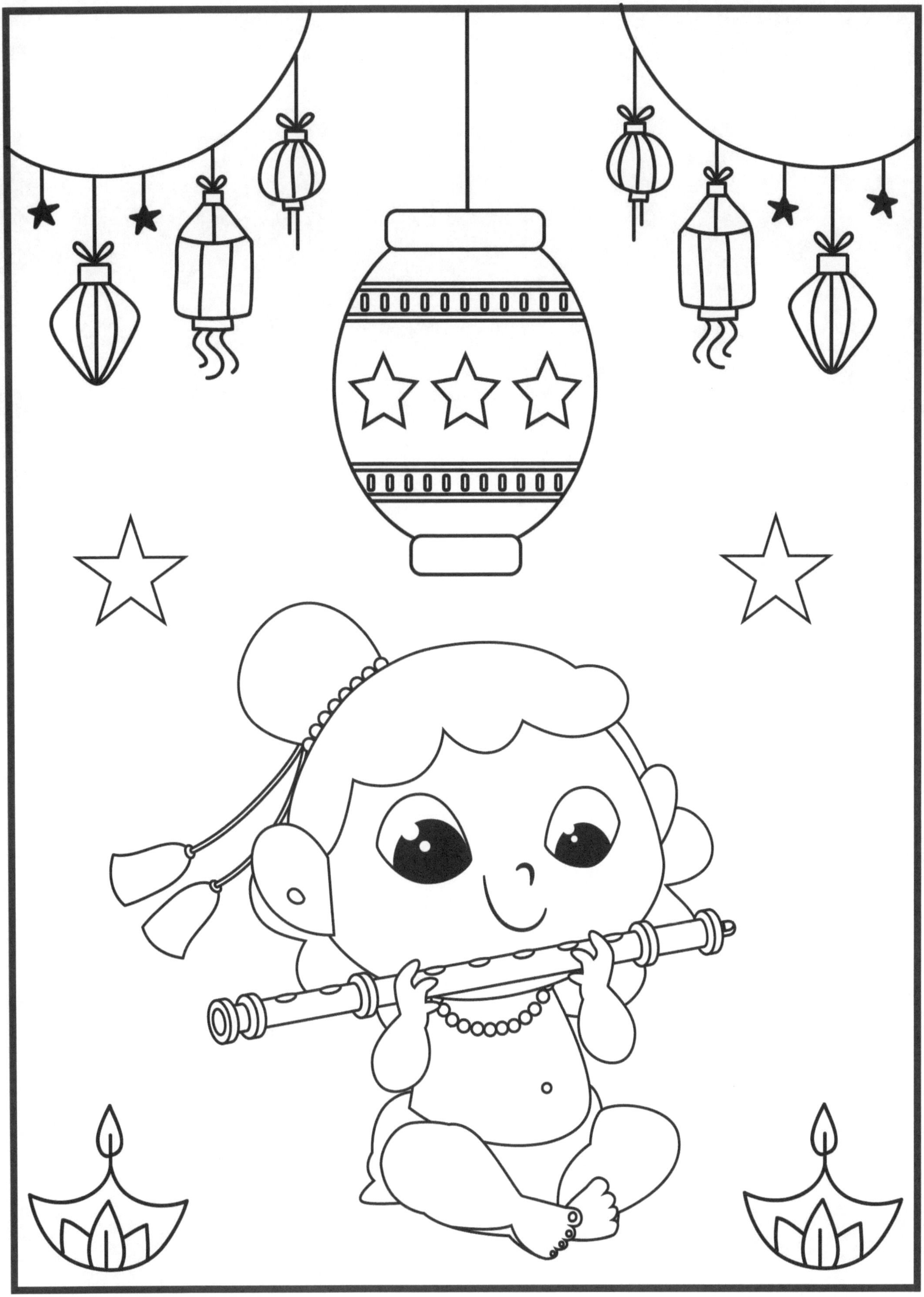

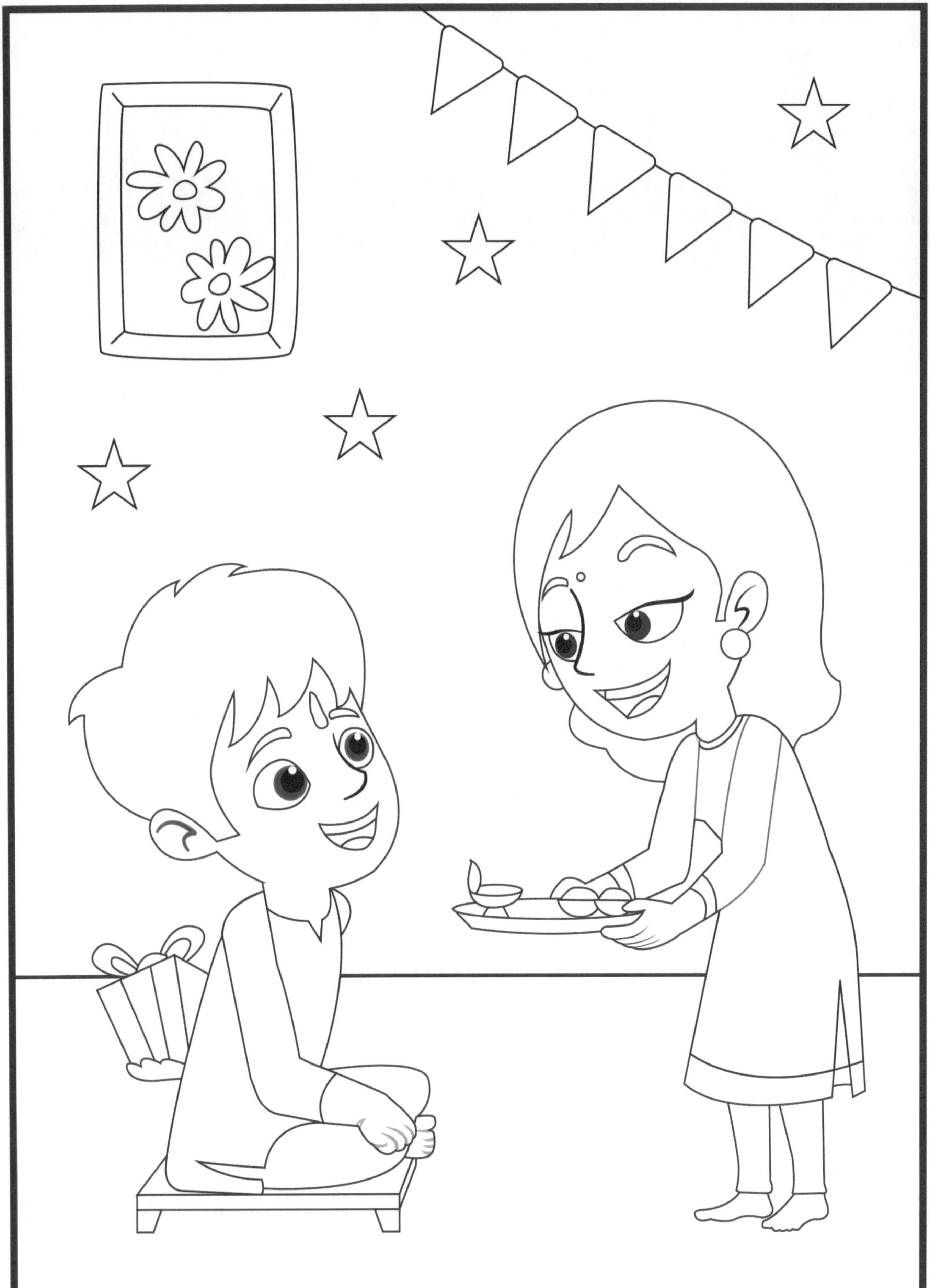

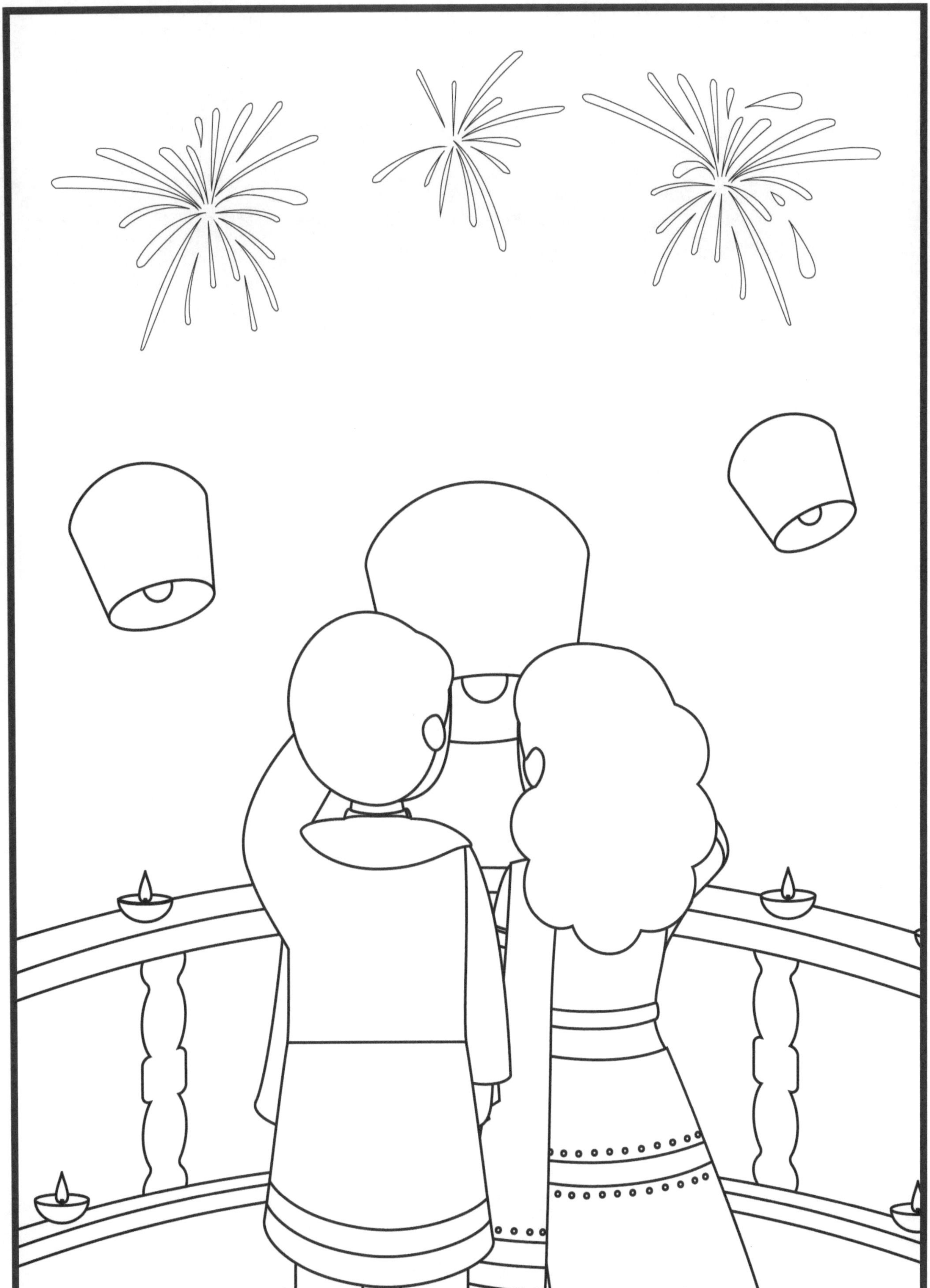

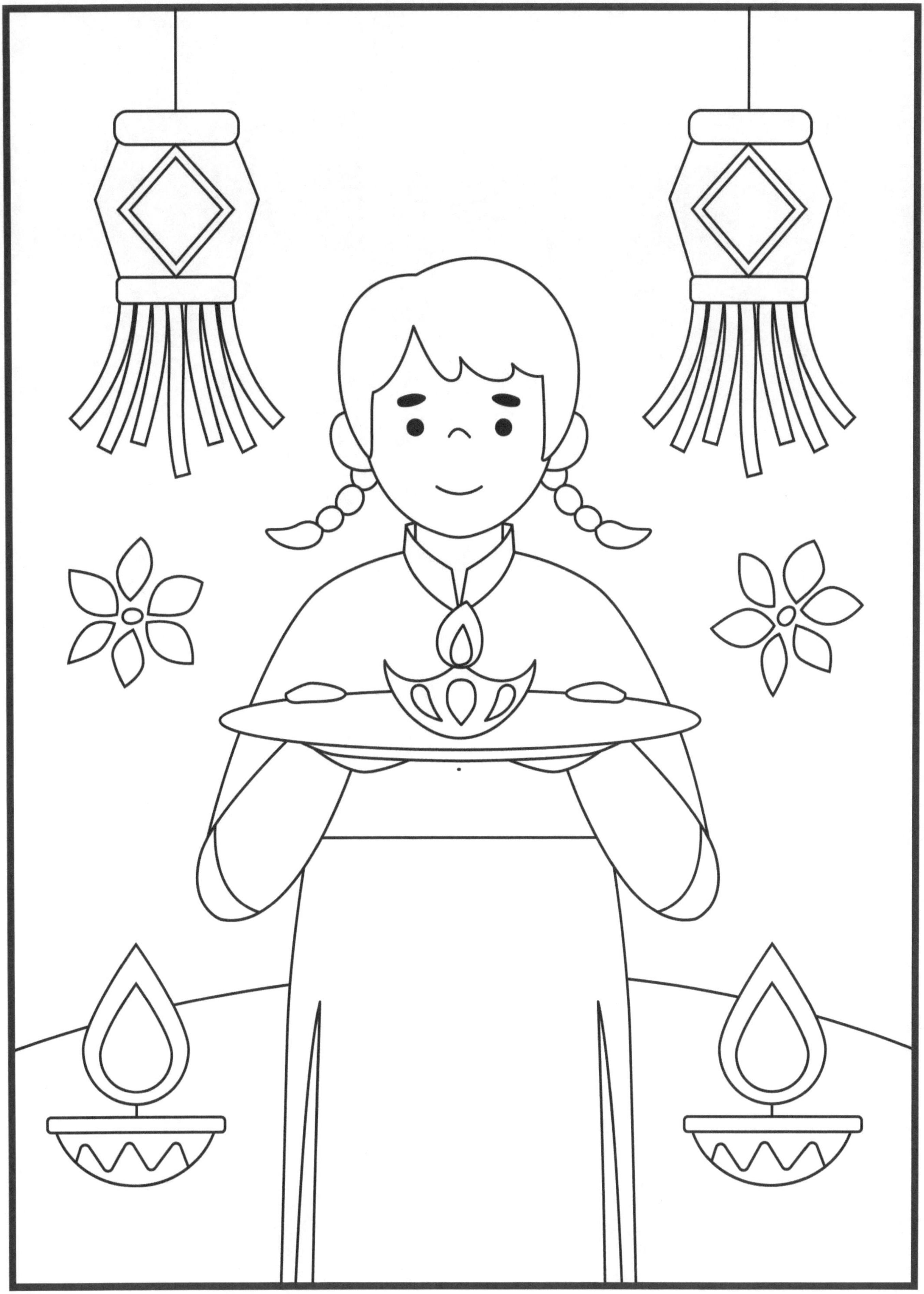

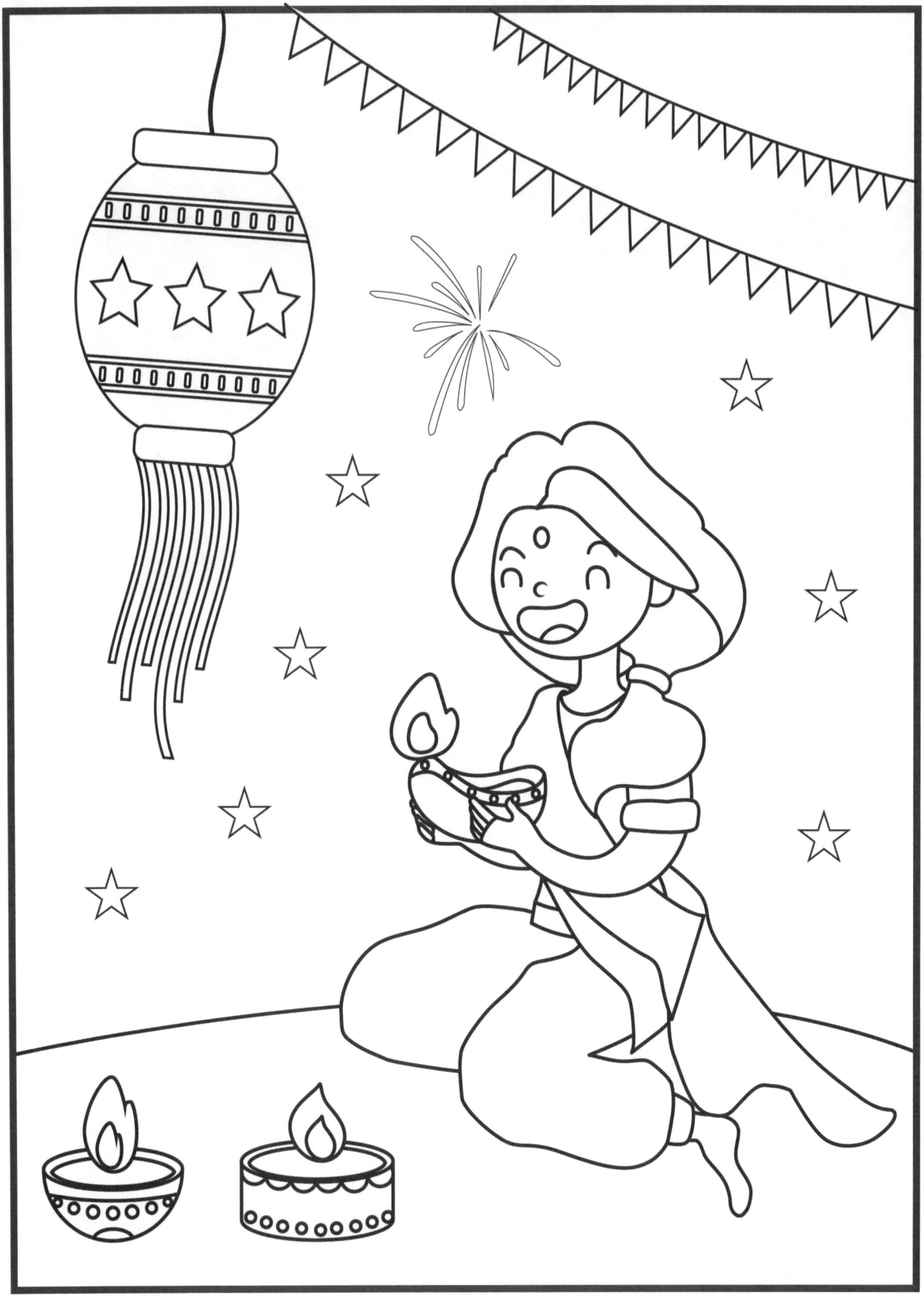

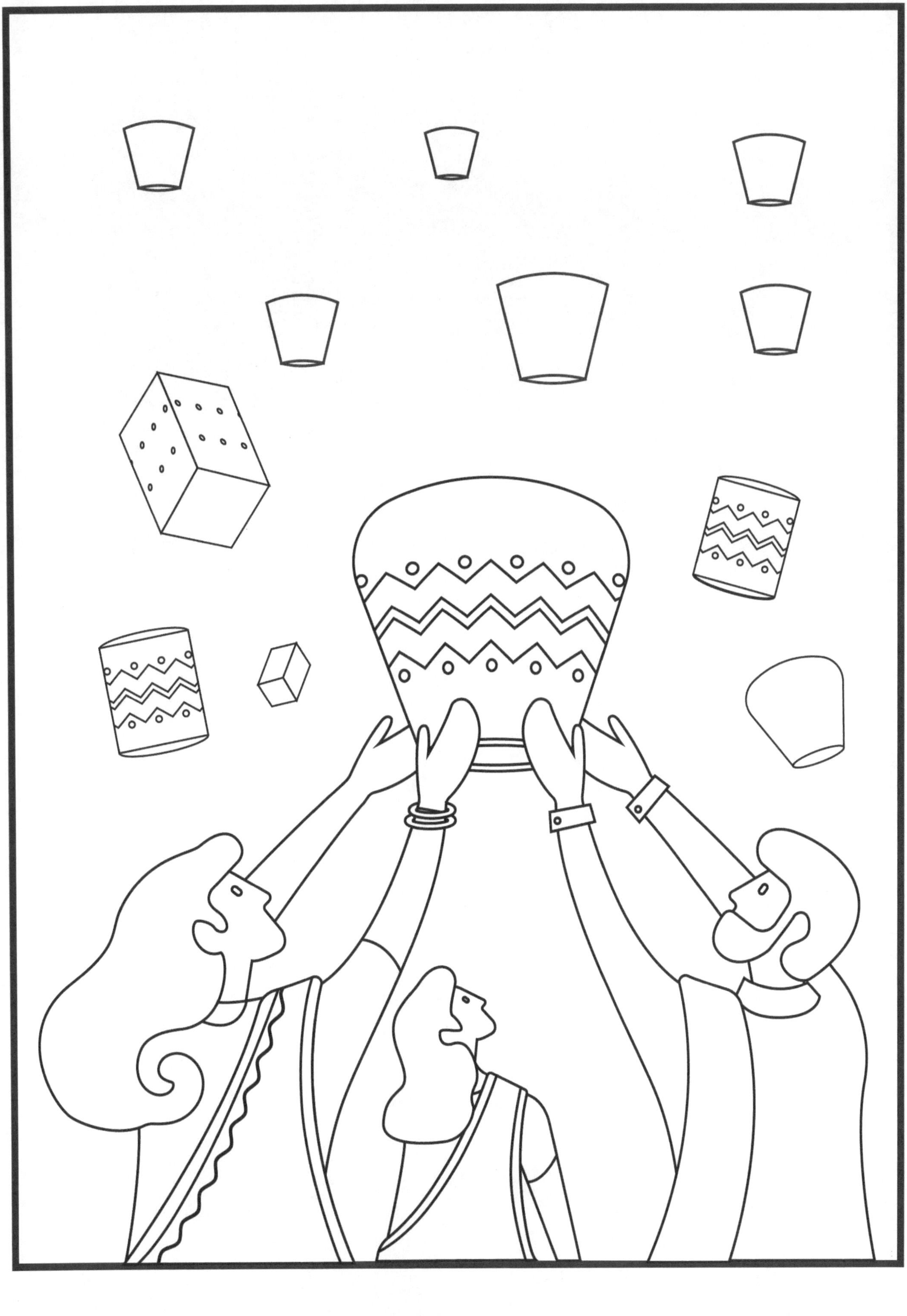

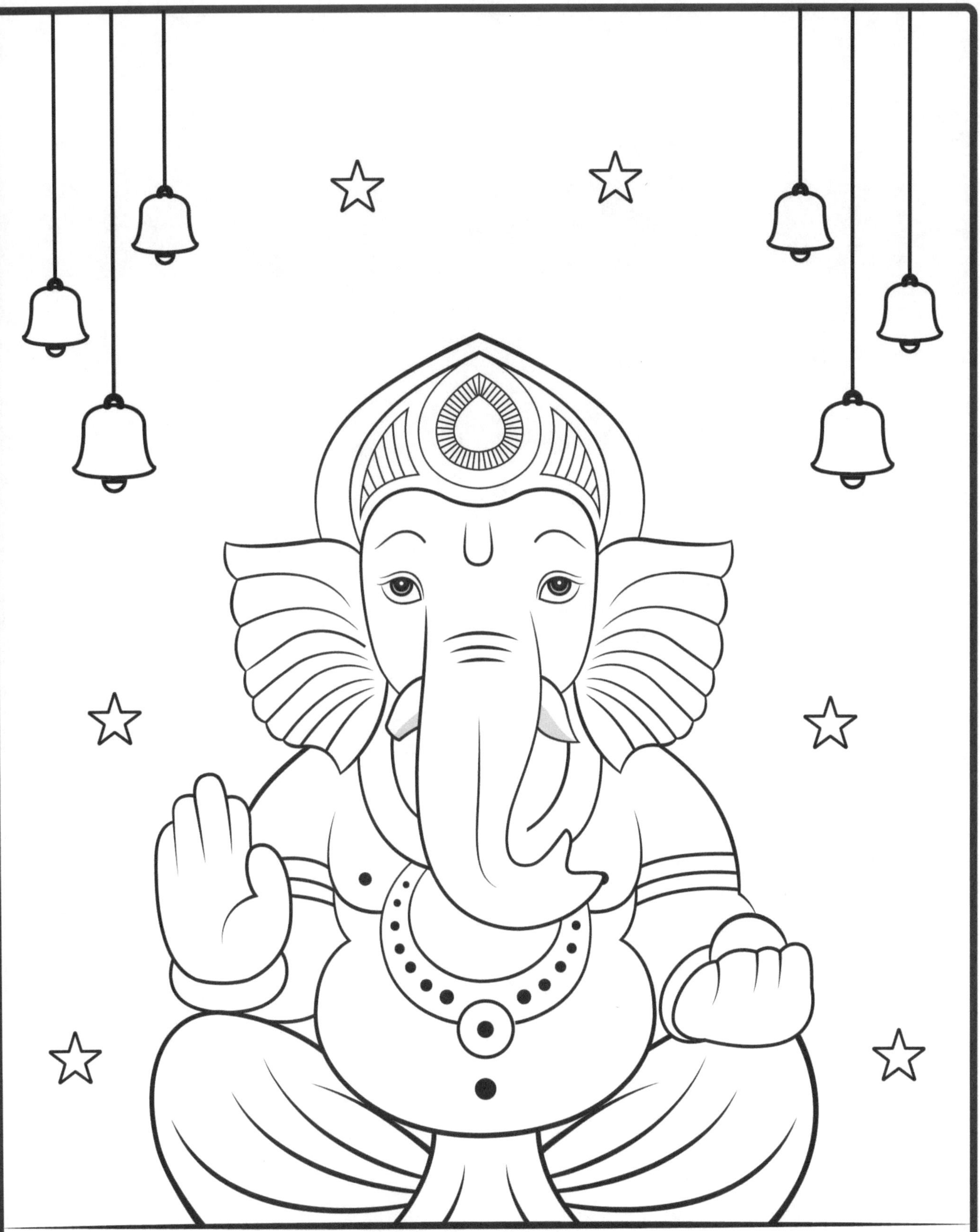

HAPPY DIWALI

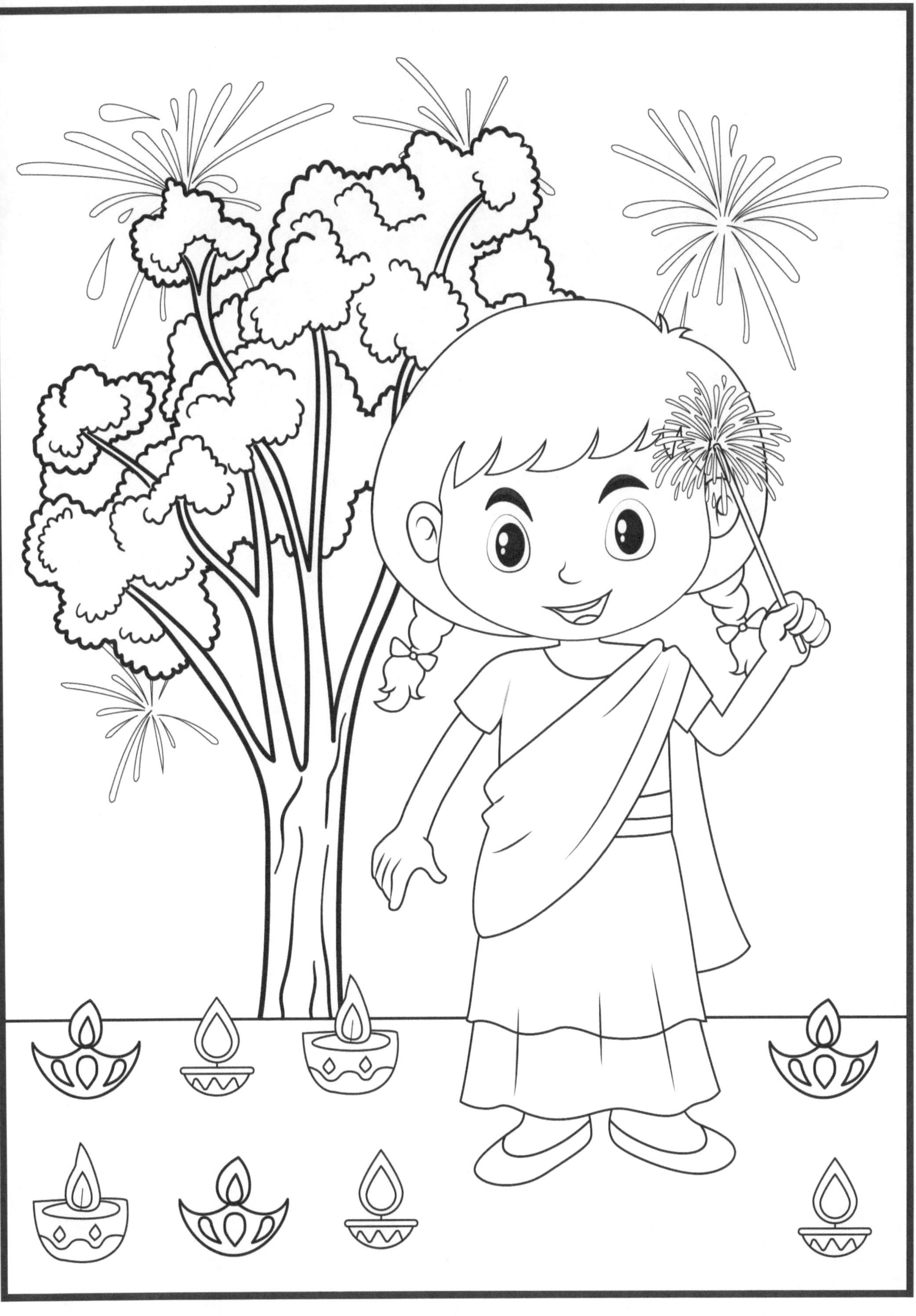

Made in United States
Troutdale, OR
10/28/2024

24183999R00046